The Atlanta Journal-Constitution

HANK

1934-2021

A Tribute to the Hammer

AARON

The Atlanta Journal-Constitution

A COX ENTERPRISES COMPANY

Donna B. Hall, Publisher
Bala Sundaramoorthy, Vice President and General Manager
Kevin G. Riley, Editor
Amy Chown, Vice President, Marketing
Mark A. Waligore, Managing Editor and Senior Director
Shawn McIntosh, Managing Editor/News
Chris Vivlamore, Sports Editor
Sandra Brown, Visuals Editor
Leo Willingham and Sandi West, Contributors

This book is available in quantity at special discounts for your group or organization.
For further information, contact:

Triumph Books LLC
814 North Franklin Street
Chicago, Illinois 60610
Phone: (312) 337-0747
www.triumphbooks.com

Printed in U.S.A.
ISBN: 978-1-62937-938-8

Content packaged by Mojo Media, Inc.
Joe Funk: Editor
Jason Hinman: Creative Director

Front cover photo by AP Images

Back cover photo by Curtis Compton / The Atlanta Journal-Constitution

CONTENTS

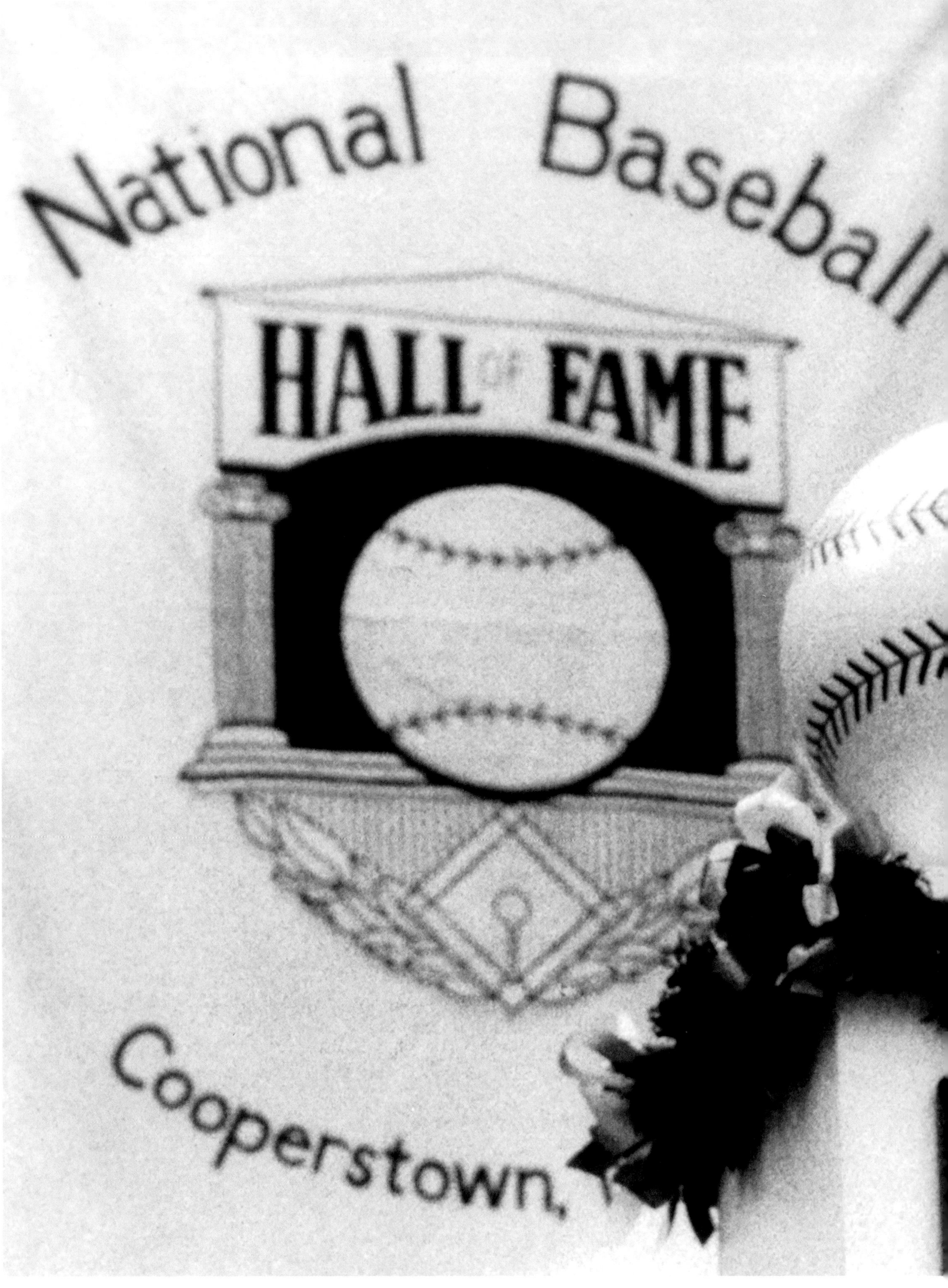
National Baseball
HALL OF FAME
Cooperstown,

Hank Aaron addresses the crowd in Cooperstown, N.Y., at his Baseball Hall of Fame induction ceremony on August 1, 1982. (Calvin Cruce/The Atlanta Journal-Constitution)

FOREWORD

By Chipper Jones

I have been blessed to know Hank Aaron for 30 and a half years of my life. I could probably tell you every word of every conversation I ever had with the man. That's how much I respected him. That's how special he was.

I honestly think he was the main reason the Atlanta Braves drafted me with the first pick in 1990. Bobby Cox can say, "Oh yeah, Chip was my first choice." I'm not buying it. And to be honest with you, I don't blame him because if I'm the general manager, I would have wanted a big flame-throwing right-hander like Todd Van Poppel myself. But from all the people I've talked to who were in the Braves draft room, Hank was adamant about them drafting me, and that means a lot. I've always tried to prove to him that I was worthy.

The first time I met him was right after I got drafted when I came up to Atlanta Fulton-County Stadium and met everybody in the front office. I was in awe. You shake his hand, and his hand just engulfs yours. I'm 6-foot-3, 230 pounds now, and I've got pretty big hands, but he had quarterback hands, like somebody you'd expect to see gripping a football. The bat looks small in his hands.

Whenever I shook his hand it was "Mr. Aaron." I can sit here now and call him "Hank" and "Henry" or "Hammer," but face to face, trust me, I gave him every bit of respect he deserved.

Over the years whenever I would see him in the clubhouse or at spring training, I would give him the courtesy of greeting him, but I was not going to bother him. If he started a conversation with me when I greeted him, I was all in, but you knew everybody was asking for their 30 seconds or their minute or their five minutes, and you never wanted to be a burden on him.

A lot of times I tried to stay out of Hank's way, but when he made himself available in spring training, I wasn't going to pass that up. I was going to be a sponge and ask questions. I was going to use this resource to my advantage.

Those conversations were just gospel. They mean so much to me, like the conversation we had about bats, how they were weighted and why he preferred them a certain way. I swung a 35-inch, 34-ounce bat, a big bat, especially in today's game. He swung just as big a bat. He had those big ol' forearms for a reason. He was whipping that thing through there. The old-school guys liked some weight in their bat, and Hank wasn't any different.

One time early in my career I asked him if he was ever intimidated when he walked to the plate. I mean, he was facing guys like Gibson, Koufax,

Hank Aaron and Atlanta Braves third baseman Chipper Jones share a moment at Turner Field in April 2004 during a ceremony commemorating the 30th anniversary of Aaron's milestone 715th career home run. (Louie Favorite/The Atlanta Journal-Constitution)

Drysdale. He said, "Chipper, I fear no man when I have a bat in my hand."

You don't know how much that conversation meant to me. From that moment on, I knew I needed to start thinking that way. No matter what the name is on the front of the jersey, no matter what the name or number is on the back of the jersey, if you throw it over that plate, I'm going to whack it. That was where my mentality and my mental approach started to take shape – and that was because of Hank.

I watched so many at-bats of his through the years. He never stepped out of the batter's box. People would throw high and tight. He would just turn his shoulder and turn back around and take a couple practice swings and get ready for the next pitch. He was the epitome of confidence in the box. His mentality was, "If you throw it over these 17 inches and I got you timed up, I'm going to hit this ball 450 feet and there's nothing you can do about it."

He's the greatest player I've ever laid eyes on, and he's in the top two or three of the greatest human beings I've ever come in contact with. He just had this peaceful ease about him, and I don't know where it came from or how he attained it. To experience some of the vitriol and the hatred he experienced through the years, for him to be as gentle and have this smile that made you feel at ease, it's amazing to me. Quite frankly, built the way I'm built, treated the way he was treated, I'd probably have an ax to grind, but you didn't ever see that with Hank.

I was asked quite a bit in the days after he passed to describe Henry Aaron in one word. The word that always came to my mind was beautiful. "The swing, the smile and the spirit, all beautiful" was the way I put it in the speech I gave at Hank's memorial service. When I was up at the podium that day, I got choked up when I got to "smile" and "spirit" because those are the parts of him that I knew, and I knew I wasn't going to be able to experience them anymore.

I never got to actually see the swing in real time, but 3,700 hits, 755 homers 2,300 RBIs – give me a break. Yeah, the swing was good, it was beautiful, I get it. But I actually got to experience the smile and the spirit and know how beautiful that was.

For everything he's done for civil rights, for social injustice, I don't know that any athlete has ever done more for their sport or for their society than Hank Aaron. He is the greatest baseball player I've ever known and the greatest humanitarian I've ever known. There will never be another Hank. ◗

As told to Carroll Rogers Walton

Hank Aaron made his Major League Baseball debut in 1954, playing for the Milwaukee Braves for 12 seasons before the Braves relocated to Atlanta in 1966. (AP Photo)

INTRODUCTION

The numbers alone boggle the mind, certifying the on-the-field greatness of Henry Louis Aaron.

The 755 home runs, for 33 years officially the most in Major League Baseball history and still the most in the eyes of many people.

The 3,771 hits, more than anyone except Pete Rose and Ty Cobb, enough that Aaron would be in the 3,000-hit club even without any of his home runs.

The 2,297 RBIs, the most in MLB history, 83 more than runner-up Babe Ruth.

The 6,856 total bases, the most in history, 722 more than runner-up Stan Musial.

The .305 career batting average, the three Gold Gloves, the 240 stolen bases and the 23 big-league seasons without once striking out 100 times, a feat Aaron himself treasured.

But the numbers, as historic and awe-inspiring as they are, do a totally inadequate job of measuring the greatness of Henry Louis Aaron and what he meant to Atlanta, the nation and beyond.

"Hank Aaron was a great baseball player, but he was an even better human being," said Ralph Garr, Aaron's former teammate in the Braves' outfield and his friend of more than 50 years. "We just want the world to know how wonderful a man he was, other than being a remarkable baseball player."

The world knows, judging from the profound outpouring of love and emotion after Aaron died in his sleep on Jan. 22, 2021 at age 86.

Aaron arrived in Atlanta with the Braves, formerly of Milwaukee, in 1966. Atlanta truly hit a home run. Not only did the city land a major league baseball team, its first big-league sports franchise, the Deep South's first big-league sports franchise, but Atlanta had the extraordinarily good fortune to land the one team that had Hank Aaron on it.

Aaron was Atlanta's first big-league sports star, and more than a half-century later, the city has never had one to equal him – on or off the field.

At Aaron's funeral, Andrew Young – civil rights leader, former United Nations ambassador and former Atlanta mayor – recalled a parade that welcomed the Braves to the city 55 years earlier. He remembered overhearing the conversation of "a bunch of country boys who happened not to be my color" as Aaron, already a baseball superstar, rode by in the back seat of a convertible. One of them said to his buddies, "You know, that fella is going to have to be able to buy a home anywhere he wants to in this town. We got to be a big-league city now."

"Just (Aaron's) presence, before he got a hit, changed this city," Young said. "… We probably wouldn't be nearly what we are if the Braves hadn't moved here and

Hank Aaron, shown here in 1968, still holds Major League Baseball records for career RBIs and total bases. (AP Photo)

brought Henry Louis Aaron with them."

Dr. Valerie Montgomery Rice, the president and dean of the Morehouse School of Medicine, described Aaron as "a man of character, integrity, generosity and kindness, an icon, a true icon."

"The world knows Hank Aaron as a trailblazing athlete, a man who faced incredible odds as he beat Babe Ruth's home run record. But to Morehouse School of Medicine, and to me, he was all that and much more," she said. "He was a stellar citizen, a businessperson, an advocate, a philanthropist, a mentor and our friend."

Aaron was the rare sports star who remained every bit as important to his city in the decades after his last game as at the height of his playing career. He became more important, even.

He played for the Braves for 21 seasons, 12 in Milwaukee and nine in Atlanta. In the Braves' first season in Atlanta, he led the National League in home runs with 44, matching his famous uniform number, and RBIs with 127. In 1969, he again hit 44 home runs as the Braves won the National League West championship. In 1971, at age 37, he hit a career-high 47 homers.

And at 9:07 p.m. on April 8, 1974, at age 40, he hit a 1-0 fastball from Los Angeles Dodgers pitcher Al Downing over the left-center field fence at Atlanta Stadium (later renamed Atlanta-Fulton County Stadium). It was the 715th home run of Aaron's career, breaking Ruth's record after a pursuit that had consumed baseball and engulfed the Braves.

"The thing that always amazed me, particularly in hindsight, is that during that time Hank was always so gracious," said Bob Hope, the Braves' public relations director at the time and a pallbearer at Aaron's funeral. "We had an incredible influx of media, just a mob of media following him around the country, as he chased the record. All the way through that process, we used to think that if it had been anybody else, there would have been problems. But with Hank, he was just gracious.

"In fact, I remember going into the clubhouse one day, exhausted. And he sat me down and said, 'Just relax now. It's just baseball.'"

To this day, and probably forever, Aaron's 715th home run remains the biggest moment in Atlanta sports history.

It was a moment, of course, that transcended sports.

"Hank Aaron was an agent of change in our society," MLB Commissioner Rob Manfred said at a memorial service for Aaron at Truist Park. "As he chased Babe Ruth's record, he received vile, racist threats. Through that wrenching period, he courageously demonstrated the strength to keep going. He persevered and delivered to all African-Americans an accomplishment in which they could take great pride. He also delivered to his racist detractors the message that greatness – greatness in a man from the Deep South, a Black man from the Deep South – could not be suppressed.

"Just as Jackie Robinson was the perfect person to change our game forever in 1947, Hank Aaron was the perfect person to meet the historic moment that he created in 1974."

The 1974 season was Aaron's last as a player for the Braves. (He wrapped up his playing career back in Milwaukee with the Brewers, then an American League team, in 1975 and 1976, mostly as a designated hitter.) But all these decades later, the Braves bask in the glory of having been Hank Aaron's team.

"He's a guy who in most ways, in every way, basically is the Braves," said Derek Schiller, the team's president and CEO. "Our brand and our team are who we are because of Hank Aaron. I know there are a lot of guys who have worn the uniform, but none like Hank, obviously."

After the 1976 season with the Brewers, Aaron retired as a player and returned to Atlanta for a very full rest-of-his-life.

As former President Bill Clinton put it: "When he retired from baseball, instead of becoming the man who used to be Hank Aaron, he just chased other dreams."

In his roles as a Hall of Fame player, a Braves executive, a Turner Broadcasting executive and board member, an entrepreneur in the automobile and restaurant businesses, a civil rights leader, a philanthropist and a founder of the "Chasing the Dream" foundation, Hank Aaron always made a difference.

"We all talk about the numbers – the home runs, the stats – but I tell you the man off the field was incredible," said former Braves outfielder Marquis Grissom, who was a college student when he first met Aaron and got treasured advice from him. "There is no other athlete that I know that had (such) an impact on my life and many other kids right here in the city of Atlanta to get them to that next level."

"He did everything the right way," Braves manager Brian Snitker said.

It is a remarkable legacy, that of a man who achieved so much on the field and still exceeded it off the field.

"In my humble opinion, he was no doubt the greatest player of our generation," said former MLB Commissioner Bud Selig, a friend of Aaron's for more than 60 years. "But more important, he was a great and wonderful human being. Neither fame nor fortune changed his extraordinary kindness and empathy, which led to his greatness off the field.

"His impact, not only on baseball but on all of America, will never be forgotten." ●

Tim Tucker, Staff Writer
The Atlanta Journal-Constitution

The sun sets over Hank Aaron's statue at Turner Field in Atlanta on November 11, 2013, the day the Braves announced the team's move from Atlanta to the suburbs of Cobb County. (Ben Gray/The Atlanta Journal-Constitution)

A GREAT PLAYER, A GREATER MAN

Aaron's Willpower and Grace Remembered

By Mark Bradley | January 22, 2021

We think of him in that moment, that Monday night in April, NBC and Curt Gowdy on hand, Al Downing throwing, the bat whipping the ball high and deep, Bill Buckner attempting to scale the fence in left-center, the ball settling into Tom House's glove in the bullpen, more than 50,000 people in the stands and millions more around the world having seen history of many sorts – sports history, sure, but also U.S. history and world history – being made. It remains the greatest moment in the annals of Atlanta sports. It's on every 10-best list of significant sports moments.

April 8, 1974, 9:07 p.m. Eastern time: Hank Aaron hit his 715th home run, eclipsing Babe Ruth's longstanding record. That moment has now outlived its author; indeed, every obituary worldwide this weekend will refer to the moment in its first paragraph, if not its first sentence. It was the moment that changed the headline on Hank Aaron's life, but the man himself was far more than any moment, even that gargantuan one. He wasn't just a hitter of homers, a grown-up playing a kid's game. He was a man who lived his life as if he knew one day he would have such a moment. By the time it arrived, he was more than ready for it.

He was a man of willpower, a man of grace. He was a Black man who grew up in the South. He faced slurs and discrimination growing up. He faced more slurs as he began to close in on the beloved Babe. He could have lashed back. He didn't. He would remember the slurs all his life – how could he not? But what we remember about Henry Louis Aaron is how he managed to rise above the insults, how he led life on his terms, how he, like Jackie Robinson before him, proved that there was more to a Black man than athletic grace. There also was an inner grace that made Aaron, again like Robinson, the absolute right man at the absolute right time.

Roger Maris' hair began to fall out during the summer of '61, the one when he chased Ruth's other great record. Aaron's pursuit of 715 was frazzled – lots of press, lots of hate mail, a whole offseason separating Nos. 713 and 714 – but the man whose greatest asset as a player was his matchless consistency didn't allow the tumult around him to become a tumult within him. He was the guy who'd flown under the radar until deep into his career, playing not for the New York Yankees (like Mickey Mantle) or the ex-New York Giants (like Willie Mays). Aaron worked in Milwaukee and then Atlanta. He first graced the cover of Sports Illustrated on Aug. 16, 1969. He was 35, then in his 16th big-league season.

Wednesday, July 16, 1969: A 13-year-old who liked sports had made the trek up the Ohio River to watch

Hank Aaron speaks during a 2007 ceremony in Milwaukee where a commemorative plaque that marks the landing spot of Aaron's 755th career home run in 1976 was unveiled. (AP Photo)

the Reds at Crosley Field. The kid had brought a ball for players to sign. The gaggle of autograph-seekers began to disperse after the Reds took batting practice, so there were only a few left when the first Brave emerged. He was smoking a cigarette. The kid from Kentucky – and nobody else – recognized him. "Hey, Henry," the kid said, "How about an autograph?" The man obliged and then moved on the field. The only autograph signed that night by one of the greatest players ever sits in a plastic case on a shelf 15 feet from where I'm typing.

Superstardom came late to Aaron, who made the All-Star team in each of his big-league seasons except the first and last. The world came to know him because of his home runs, but home runs weren't really what made him a great player. He never hit more than 47 in a single season. He batted .301 at age 39. He never struck out 100 times in a year. And here's the best Aaron stat: If you took away his 755 home runs, he'd still have had 3,016 hits.

I apologize. On the day Henry Aaron died, we shouldn't be playing fun with numbers. (Although, you must admit, his make for great fun.) He was bigger than his biggest moment, more than his fattest number. His temperament and his surpassing skills made him the only man to take that historic swing. He left all those expressing vitriol because he happened to be Black looking the way such cretins deserve to look. He never gave in to the hatred, never lashed back. He kept on keeping on. He led a long, full life.

To borrow the title from the autobiography he wrote with the late Lonnie Wheeler, he had a hammer. He was Hammerin' Hank, great player, great Atlantan, great man. As we mourn his passing, we must also recognize the reality: We were, and we remain, ennobled by his life. ●

On the eve of his 80th birthday in 2014, Hank Aaron sits in the living room of his Atlanta home. (Curtis Compton/ The Atlanta Journal-Constitution)

NOW AND FOREVER

Mr. Hank Aaron: The One True Home Run King

By Steve Hummer | January 22, 2021

Everything written or said about Mr. Aaron – neither Henry nor Hank to me, but Mr. Aaron – has spoken to the best part of ourselves. A part we have too often misplaced. That part where understanding and grace and strength of character still hold out.

A million words have been spent trying to define a life of great meaning. And everything has been so aptly put – with one glaring exception.

From the AJC: "Aaron, at one time baseball's all-time home run king, died Friday at the age of 86."

From the New York Times: "Hank Aaron, who faced down racism as he eclipsed Babe Ruth as baseball's home run king, hitting 755 homers and holding the most celebrated record in sports for more than 30 years, has died. He was 86."

From MLB.com: "Aaron passed Ruth on the all-time home run list on April 8, 1974, at age 40. ... He was baseball's home run king for 33 years."

These tributes to Mr. Aaron all come with the mistaken claim that he was, not is, the home run king. The error is in giving blind obedience to a number rather than obeying the heart. There are those of us who never will concede that he doesn't still hold the most cherished mark in baseball.

Not when 755 always will carry far more significance than whatever number Barry Bonds posted. OK, fine, it was 762, not that it resonates in any way.

In this monarchy, the people crown who they please. And the crown belongs squarely on a head that didn't grow several sizes during some biochemistry experiment gone mad.

Mr. Aaron wouldn't care to have his accomplishments burnished by tearing down another player. He was a better man than that. But I can't say the same for myself.

When Bonds passed Mr. Aaron's 755 in 2007, the moment naturally lacked all the greater racial and social ramifications of passing Babe Ruth in 1974. But it also lacked the air of authenticity. It was abundantly clear that Bonds had pumped himself up on performance enhancers – the same certainty that keeps him out of the Hall of Fame today – while we know that Mr. Aaron's record was as all-natural as sunshine itself.

On the night Bonds hit No. 756, Aaron said in a taped message, "I'll move over now and offer my best wishes to Barry and his family on this historical achievement. My hope today, as it was on that April evening in 1974, is that the achievement of this record will inspire others to chase their own dreams."

Hank Aaron holds aloft the ball moments after he hit his 715th home run in Atlanta on April 8, 1974. (File Photo/ The Atlanta Journal Constitution)

He never would condemn Bonds with anywhere near the volume or vitriol of his most zealous fans. Why would a man who had to wade through so much ugliness to get to his record willingly get into the mud again to defend it?

Mr. Aaron's death has given reason once more to put him in Bonds' shady company. The sin is that there is any need to invoke Bonds' name at all in the same breath. But at least the comparison makes the far better man seem even better.

Of the stories considering again where these two stand in baseball's collective conscience, the most scathing by far came from Jeff Pearlman, a Bonds biographer. The headline of the piece in Deadspin leaves no room for interpretation: "Hank Aaron was everything, Barry Bonds was nothing."

To his way of thinking, it is clear-cut. There is Mr. Aaron. And there is the Anti-Aaron.

In part, Pearlman writes:

"Hank Aaron went out of his way to make the lives of those around him better. Barry Bonds went out of his way to make the lives of those around him more difficult. He had a perverse way of rejoicing when others struggled."

And of the record-breaking night, he adds:

"Then, on Aug. 7, 2007, Bonds hit his 756th home run – a cartoonishly juiced man 'making history' even though history shrugged. I was there the night the mark was broken, and while the fans went crazy and Bonds' family members engulfed him in hugs, it was akin to complimenting a person with gobs of plastic surgery how young she looks."

While we mourn Mr. Aaron, it is unnecessary now to pile on Bonds any further. That serves no purpose other than to darken the celebration of this life. Still, it seems the right time to serve one reminder.

There is but one home run king, now and forever. And you may call him Hank or Henry or Mr. Aaron. ◗

Hank Aaron shows off his famous baseball stance. (Curtis Compton/The Atlanta Journal-Constitution)

A TRANSCENDENT FIGURE

Hank Aaron Memorialized as Towering Presence On and Off Field

By Steve Hummer | January 26, 2021

Hank Aaron lived a life of legend. Now upon his death comes the hard, nearly impossible, duty of others to speak on it and attempt to do it justice.

Oh, how they tried Tuesday, honoring a man who Major League Baseball commissioner Rob Manfred said, "belongs on our sport's Mount Rushmore; he stood on and off the field above all others."

On this day the long goodbye to Aaron took the form of a memorial service at the current Braves ballpark a county away from where he broke Babe Ruth's home run record almost 47 years ago, the shot heard throughout humanity. Aaron died in his sleep Friday morning at the age of 86.

Pick up Tuesday's tributes there, again in Manfred's words: "(Aaron) delivered to his racist detractors the message that greatness – greatness in a man from the Deep South, a Black man from the Deep South – could not be suppressed. Just as Jackie Robinson was the perfect person to change our game forever in 1947, Hank Aaron was the perfect person to meet the historic moment that he created in 1974."

At Truist Park, a large green No. 44 – Aaron's number – stood out vividly against the outfield grass wearing its winter beige. Back where they honor the Braves past, in an alcove just beyond the home plate that Aaron set in place in 2016 before the park's opening the next spring, a roster of important people gathered to speak of Aaron's greater importance.

It was no task to take lightly. "It's so scary standing up here; I respected the man so much I wouldn't want to disappoint him or his family," Braves Hall of Fame third baseman Chipper Jones said.

On Tuesday, Braves Chairman Terry McGuirk presided over the memorial. Tributes, both in person and on video, followed from Manfred, Negro League Museum President Bob Kendrick, players past (Jones, fellow Hall of Famers Tom Glavine and John Smoltz, Dale Murphy, Marquis Grissom) and players present (Freddie Freeman). Braves manager Brian Snitker fought through the emotion of once more retelling the story of how much he owed Aaron. For it was while Aaron oversaw the Braves' minor league system that he redirected a young catcher whose modest talents were taking him nowhere and gave him his first job managing.

It has been a hard 10 months for a Braves lifer like the 65-year-old Snitker, who has watched pillar upon pillar of his franchise fall. First Bill Bartholomay, who brought the team to Atlanta from Milwaukee, died in March. Then in the last month, Hall of Fame

Hank Aaron speaks with minor league players in West Palm Beach, Florida, in 1987. Upon his retirement after the 1976 season, he joined the Braves' front office as Vice President and Director of Player Development. (Joey Ivansco/ The Atlanta Journal-Constitution)

knuckleballer Phil Niekro and long-time Braves announcer and Hall of Fame pitcher Don Sutton died. And now, Aaron's death, the loss deeply personal.

"I'll miss the friend and the mentor that I had in my life," Snitker said, voice breaking.

"We've lost a great friend," he added.

There will be more stories to tell and more tears to shed at 1 p.m. Wednesday during Aaron's funeral services at Friendship Baptist Church. That, like his memorial, will be telecast by the team's lead network, Fox Sports Southeast.

Fortunately at such services, those who line up to pay homage are not constrained by the same humility that escorted Aaron through 86 exceptional years. They are free to sing praises in a voice Aaron never used.

Those who were accustomed to the company of stars spoke of how Aaron stood separately, leaving them in awe.

"I always felt like I was in the presence of greatness," Glavine said, "but was always struck by how humble Mr. Aaron was. He would never let you know that he was arguably the greatest baseball player of all time."

How great? To illustrate, the commissioner repeated a story that aptly summarized Aaron's place in the firmament of star athletes: "The great Muhammad Ali once said that Hank was the only man I idolized more than myself."

Those who have done stout work in the community – like Grissom, whose baseball academy encourages minority participation in the sport – pointed to Aaron's example of community involvement as a guiding light.

"He lit a fire in me that is still lit today," Grissom said.

"I wanted to be like him. I wanted to dream like him," he added.

Toward honoring Aaron's commitment to building minority participation through all levels of baseball,

the Braves announced Tuesday they were forming the Henry Louis Aaron Fund. McGuirk said the team would kick-start the fund with a $1 million contribution, matched in part by separate $500,000 contributions by MLB and the MLB players association.

Long after Aaron was done playing, after the last of his 755 career home runs was hit, after his 2,297 RBIs and 6,856 total bases were tallied – representing a journey of nearly 117 miles around the base paths for his 23-year career – he was a front office constant for the team. When he wasn't suggesting Snitker try this managing thing or that the team draft Jones ahead of some pitcher named Todd Van Poppel, his mere presence around the team set a standard.

"It's been an honor of a lifetime to be able to wear the same uniform that Hank Aaron wore," Murphy said during his video tribute.

"Hank's spirit permeated our whole organization. If you wanted to be a ballplayer, this is the way you play. If you want to represent your organization, this is how you act. If you want to serve your fellow man, this is what you do." ⬤

Prior to pregame ceremonies in 1999, commemorating the 25th anniversary of Hank Aaron's record-breaking 715th home run, Aaron signs autographs for Braves players Ozzie Guillen and Eddie Perez as well as coach Don Baylor. (Ben Gray/The Atlanta Journal-Constitution)

HOMEGOING

Hank Aaron's Funeral a Tribute to More Than a Baseball Great
By Steve Hummer | January 28, 2021

One final time they gathered as best they could in a period of a pandemic, presidents and pastors, family and friends, to usher Henry Louis Aaron home.

Some would call it a funeral, but the preferred term at Atlanta's Friendship Baptist Church is "homegoing." And from there, this one was televised throughout the earthly city Aaron made better.

They didn't gather so much to pay mere homage to Aaron's fluid swing and weighty baseball records. The portrait that flanked his casket was not of Aaron in a ballplayer's uniform, but of an older man in a light brown suit looking hopefully heavenward. The images that flashed on the screen at the very start weren't of his triumphs of 23 seasons with the Milwaukee and Atlanta Braves and the Milwaukee Brewers, but rather those of Americans craving social justice, from black-and-white photos dating to the 1960s to George Floyd and the Black Lives Matter movement of today.

Baseball, and Aaron's famed 715th home run that passed Babe Ruth in 1974, mainly served as a convenient platform from which to broaden his legacy.

"It's interesting that he was so protective of baseball and its integrity," former President Bill Clinton said from the rostrum. "I think one reason was that despite all the racism and all the threats and all the terrible things that happened to him when he was about to break (Ruth's) home run record, he knew that when he was playing, baseball was on the level.

"If you were an African-American when Hank Aaron was young ... and even now in too many places, there are still so many days when people wonder if anything will ever be on the level again. Baseball did that for him. Amidst all the racism, nobody fooled with his numbers.

"He treated other people like he knew they wanted and deserved the same thing, whether they could play baseball or not. He wanted everybody to have their baseball, some way to be on the level. To be seen as who they were, to be judged for what they were. That's his legacy to me."

Born in Mobile, Alabama, Aaron will be eternally Atlanta's, laid to rest at the South-View Cemetery at the south end of town.

For this is a city Aaron helped change when the Braves moved here in 1966. That is the reckoning of civil rights leader, former mayor and former U.N. Ambassador Andrew Young.

Young recalled the day the new team paraded through town, when he overheard "a bunch of country boys who happened to not be my color."

As Aaron passed aboard a convertible, one of them

Former President Bill Clinton was one of several speakers giving tribute to Hank Aaron's remarkable life at his funeral service on Jan. 27, 2021 at Friendship Baptist Church in Atlanta. (AP Photo)

said to his buddies, "You know, that fella is going to have to be able to buy a home anywhere he wants to in this town. We got to be a big-league city now."

"Just his presence before he ever got a hit changed this city," Young said.

One after another they came forth Wednesday to illuminate the other facets of the home run king.

Aaron was a constant on the field – hitting 20 or more home runs for 20 consecutive seasons, never striking out more than 97 times in a season. "Spring would come, the trees would blossom, the birds would chirp and Aaron would begin wearing out the pitchers. It was a blessing," Clinton said.

Yet that was but a hint of how Aaron would lead his life for the 44 years after his retirement.

Aaron's funeral, Clinton said, "was a tribute to a consistent life of caring and doing and being a certain way."

Not a single ballplayer spoke. Rather, precious time was reserved for Dr. Valerie Montgomery Rice, the president and dean of the Morehouse School of Medicine. She spoke of the millions the Aarons have given the school, and the student pavilion named after Aaron's wife, Billye.

"The world knows Hank Aaron as a trailblazing athlete, a man who faced incredible odds as he beat Babe Ruth's home run record. But to Morehouse School of Medicine he was all that and much more. He was a stellar citizen, a businessperson, an advocate, a philanthropist, a mentor and a friend," she said.

The former president of Sterling Motorcars, Tom Morehead, spoke of how his friend opened a BMW dealership in the late 1990s "motivated by the fact he wanted the industry to change its complexion; he wanted the complexion to look like individuals like us."

Quiana Lewis, now in a Ph.D. program at Johns Hopkins University, was chosen to speak for the hundreds of young students Aaron's Chasing The Dream Foundation has supported. "Mr. Aaron's investments

early in life provided so many youth the springboard they needed to realize their dreams," she said.

Former baseball commissioner Bud Selig recalled the day in 1957 when the New York Times juxtaposed a photo of white teammates carrying Aaron off the field after a pennant-clinching home run alongside one of Black students being set upon by police in Little Rock, Ark.

On this day, Braves chairman Terry McGuirk chose to defer all talk of Aaron's playing career. Instead he recalled Aaron's sharp, straight-edged honesty in one long-ago Turner Broadcasting board meeting when McGuirk was overselling their Braves holding. Asked what he thought, Aaron replied, "The team is so slow it will take four singles to score a run."

"That ended my presentation," McGuirk said. And, Aaron, by the way, was right, McGuirk said.

Beyond a purely seminal baseball moment, that 715th home run on the night of April 8, 1974 off the Dodgers' Al Downing "wasn't about only chasing down Babe Ruth," Hall of Fame broadcaster Bob Costas said in his video tribute. "It was about staring down some of the worst of America and prevailing as an enduring symbol about what can be best about America," he said.

Yes, Hank Aaron is undeniably on the short list of the greatest ballplayers ever. But it was how he lived after he put down his bat that was such the enduring theme of his homegoing.

"The longer life went on for Hank Aaron, the more graceful he became," Clinton said.

Then the president sent his friend off tenderly.

"Hank Aaron knew that in every heart he encountered there were scales that sometimes tilted toward darkness and sometime towards light, and the state of grace required the will and heart to tilt them toward light. And that required love." ◗

Following news of Hank Aaron's death on Jan. 22, 2021, fans left tributes at the site of the old Fulton County Stadium in Atlanta. (AP Photo)

Baseball bats that form the number 755 are part of a display near the Hank Aaron statue in Monument Garden at Truist Park, the Atlanta Braves' current stadium. (Curtis Compton/The Atlanta Journal-Constitution)

EQUAL PLAYING FIELD

How Henry Aaron Made Baseball a Form of Civil Rights Activism

By Ernie Suggs | January 22, 2021

In 1966, when the Braves relocated to Atlanta from Milwaukee, Hank Aaron was the team's biggest star, and he was reluctant to go back South.

Born and raised in deeply segregated Mobile, Alabama, Aaron had never played on a baseball field with white players prior to joining the Braves' farm system in 1952. Milwaukee became a respite from Jim Crow, but, as Aaron's biographer Howard Bryant wrote: "The family now risked having everything they'd earned in Milwaukee taken away by the denigrating ways of life in the South."

"I have lived in the South, and I don't want to live there again," Aaron said at the time. "We can go anywhere in Milwaukee. I don't know what would happen in Atlanta."

Aaron found a sprawling home in the comfortably middle-class Black enclave of southwest Atlanta and started building relationships with his neighbors and other Black figures in town – notably Andrew Young, Martin Luther King Sr., and Martin Luther King Jr.

Young recalled their first meeting, where Aaron appeared somewhat embarrassed that he had not been more involved publicly in the civil rights movement.

"Martin was a big baseball fan. We told (Aaron) not to worry," Young told The Atlanta Journal-Constitution. "We told him just keep hitting that ball. That was his job."

Young said Aaron's work on the baseball field and being the face of baseball in the Deep South was a form of civil rights activism, showing that achievements can be made if the playing field was equal.

He was a natural extension, said Young, of Joe Louis and Jackie Robinson, who directly confronted race with their bodies.

"He was like Joe Louis knocking out Max Schmeling in '38 and Jackie breaking the color line in '47," Young said. "You got to remember that Martin didn't start until '55. Baseball and Hank opened up a lot of doors in a lot of people's minds."

Aaron, who died Jan. 22, 2021 at the age of 86 in the same Atlanta home he purchased when he moved here, was known for his exploits on the field as well as his business savvy and philanthropy after he retired.

But coming of age in the 1940s and 1950s and playing baseball in a world dominated by whites, while finding his voice as an outspoken critic of racial inequality, Aaron also served as a major civil rights leader.

"Henry had never considered himself as important a historical figure as Jackie Robinson," Bryant wrote in his 2010 biography of Aaron, "The Last Hero." "And yet by twice integrating the South – first in the Sally [South Atlantic] League and later as the first Black star on the first major league team in the South (during the apex of the civil rights movement, no less) – his road

Hank Aaron celebrates with Fulton County Commissioner Reginald Eaves (left) and Jesse Jackson at campaign headquarters after Andrew Young was elected mayor of Atlanta in 1981. (Louie Favorite/The Atlanta Journal-Constitution)

in many ways was no less lonely, and in other ways far more difficult."

Aaron started his professional baseball career in the Negro American League in 1952 as an 18-year-old star of the Indianapolis Clowns. In 14 games, the 180-pound shortstop would hit .483, with 28 hits, six doubles, five home runs and 24 RBIs.

The Boston Braves quickly signed him. Until that point, Aaron had never shared the field with a white ballplayer. The team assigned him to play for an integrated farm team in Eau Claire, Wisconsin.

But for the 1953 season, the Braves promoted him to the Jacksonville, Florida, club in the South Atlantic League. Although Robinson had just completed his 6th year in the majors for the Dodgers after breaking the color barrier, the Sally League, with teams in the Deep South, had not yet integrated.

Until Aaron arrived.

Throughout towns such as Columbus and Macon, he received a constant stream of taunts. In Bryant's biography, even when he played well enough to soften up Jacksonville's home crowd, the compliments were still backhanded.

Felix Mantilla, a dark-skinned Puerto Rican who had been sent to Jacksonville to room with Aaron, recalled a moment after the two of them helped the team win a key game.

As they were leaving the ballpark, a winded fan ran up to them smiling. "I just wanted to say," the man said. "That you (racial epithets) played a hell of a game."

After his promotion to the Milwaukee Braves in 1954, just a year before the Montgomery Bus Boycotts, Aaron began to take notice of the civil rights movement and Democratic causes. In 1960, while his boyhood idol Robinson supported Richard Nixon, Aaron traveled throughout Wisconsin campaigning for John F. Kennedy.

But Bryant wrote that even when he expressed his opinions on racial matters, Aaron was always wary of being labeled a troublemaker.

"His political strategy would always begin behind closed doors," Bryant wrote.

Longtime Atlanta friend Xernona Clayton said while Aaron may not have been as visible as others, "He was someone we knew we could count for contributions or if we needed him to make a statement or an appearance somewhere where it was important to show solidarity."

After he retired, Aaron devoted his attention to business and charity, setting up programs and scholarships for Black students. In 1999, he became the first Black majority owner of a BMW franchise, and he lobbied for efforts encouraging more young Black athletes to play baseball.

In 2016, Aaron and his wife Billye Suber Aaron donated $3 million to the Morehouse School of Medicine as part of an expansion of academic facilities at the Atlanta institution. "He let people know 'I'm there with you,'" Clayton said. "He understood the pain of segregation and discrimination. He never forgot who he was and what the needs were of Black people trying to get equality and justice."

In 1999, Aaron, then a senior vice president with the Braves, said he was "very sick and disgusted" at the revelation that Braves reliever John Rocker had made homophobic and racist comments in a Sports Illustrated profile.

"I have no place in my heart for people who feel that way," Aaron said.

Rocker personally apologized to Aaron, who had seen his share of those attitudes even late into his career.

On April 4, 1974, the opening day of what would be his most memorable season, Aaron was uneasy.

He had 713 home runs, just two shy of breaking Babe Ruth's hallowed record of 714.

The Braves were opening in Cincinnati and the Reds asked him if there was anything the franchise could do for him.

"Yes," Aaron told them.

Just six years earlier to that day, Martin Luther King Jr., his friend, had been assassinated.

Hank Aaron and former Braves relief pitcher John Rocker walk out of Aaron's BMW dealership in Union City, Georgia, after a meeting in 1999. The two spoke privately for nearly 25 minutes in Aaron's glassed-in office in the showroom after Rocker made homophobic and racist comments in a Sports Illustrated profile. Aaron told Rocker a story of taking abuse from a fan during his minor league days in Macon, where Aaron broke the color barrier in the South Atlantic League. He told Rocker how he always tried to keep his reactions to himself, to lean on his teammates, to laugh about it. "The only thing that I'm giving him advice in doing is in trying to get his life back together again," Aaron said after the meeting. "What he said was very offensive. And I told him it's something that it's hard for me to forgive. But I'm glad I had the chance to talk with (him)... Who am I not to forgive?" (Marlene Karas/The Atlanta Journal-Constitution)

Aaron asked that the assassination of King be publicly acknowledged with a pregame moment of silence. In the days and months leading up to that day, Aaron had been constantly harassed by so-called fans of the Babe, who didn't want a Black man breaking the record. Letters would come in by the sack full promising Aaron the same fate that had befallen King in 1968.

The moment never happened.

In the first inning, Aaron launched his 714th homerun, tying Ruth. Four days later, on April 8 in Atlanta, he broke the record.

The Rev. Jesse Jackson, who had discussed the moment of silence idea with Aaron before the game, said Aaron was a "hero and champion against racial odds."

"He made all of us proud. With his presence, he transformed baseball and helped make it major," Jackson told The Atlanta Journal-Constitution. "He rode on the peoples' shoulders as we looked upon him in adoration. And we rode on his shoulders as he lifted us to higher heights."

Eight years earlier, on a chilly morning in early 1966, Young had stood in front of the old American hotel on what is now Spring Street. The city was throwing a parade to welcome the Braves to Atlanta, and Young found a spot behind "a bunch of folks in country overalls because I wanted to hear and see what their reactions would be to the Black players."

Each player on the team came by perched in the back seat of a convertible. Aaron was one of the last to ride through. Young listened as one of the men in overalls nudged his buddy.

"Now, if we're gonna be a big-league city, that fella's gonna have to be able to live anywhere he wants to live in this town," Young recalled.

"I said, 'They said that?' This must mean something. He was welcomed in this city and he loved this city." ◗

Staff writer Shelia Poole contributed to this story.

Boxing legend Muhammad Ali (center) was joined by Georgia state senator Leroy Johnson (left) and Hank Aaron during a 1976 press conference at the Atlanta International Hotel where Ali spoke in support of the proposed Atlanta Sports Hall of Fame. (Charles R. Pugh Jr./The Atlanta Journal-Constitution)

A HERO TO MANY

Henry Aaron Stood for Black Excellence

By Michael Cunningham | January 22, 2021

I was an infant when Braves legend Hank Aaron hit home run No. 715. My impressions of what happened April 8, 1974 at Atlanta-Fulton County Stadium were formed by repeated viewings of the famous TV highlight. My thoughts about Aaron's legacy are, believe or not, influenced by an argument among schoolmates when I was in sixth or seventh grade.

The topic: best baseball player of all time. One of my white peers picked Babe Ruth because he was the Home Run King. I told him that Aaron hit more home runs than Ruth. The classmate responded that Aaron's record was fraudulent because MLB counted homers that he hit in the minor leagues.

That wasn't true, of course. The peer also downplayed or dismissed the achievements of other Black ballplayers, but his denial of Aaron's record stuck with me. Aaron's home run total was a matter of fact. How could my classmate deny it?

It's likely that somewhere along the line, someone told him the lie about Aaron's record, and he believed it. Honestly, I started to have doubts about it when he told me. It was an early lesson in the power of the lies told to maintain the myth of white supremacy.

Falsehoods are weaponized so as to deny and downplay Black excellence achieved against great odds and animus, as Aaron did. Aaron was in the record books, but some people couldn't accept a Black man as Home Run King of American's pastime.

I thought back to that schoolyard argument when I heard the news of Aaron's death Friday morning at 86 years old. I would think about it each time I saw Aaron at Braves games, spring training or events. It increased my reverence of Aaron to know that he succeeded when some wanted him to fail just because he's Black.

"I lost a hero," said ex-Braves outfielder Brian Jordan, who was 7 years old when Aaron broke Ruth's record. "As a Black boy growing up loving the game of baseball, Hank Aaron was 'That Guy.'"

Aaron made his MLB debut in 1954, seven years after Jackie Robinson became the first Black player of the modern MLB era. By then, several other Black ballplayers had reached the majors, including Willie Mays, Roy Campanella and Larry Doby. All are members of the Hall of Fame, but none held a record as revered as the home run mark.

As Aaron closed in on the record, he faced a racist backlash that included death threats. Dusty Baker, Aaron's Braves teammate, said in a 2007 interview with NPR that Aaron didn't talk much to his teammates about the abuse. But Aaron once warned Baker and

Hank Aaron made his major league debut in 1954, seven years after Jackie Robinson became the first Black player of the modern era. (AP Photo)

outfielder Ralph Garr about sitting next to him in the dugout during a game because someone was going to shoot at him.

"It wasn't a very happy time," Baker said. "It wasn't nearly as happy as it should've been."

Lewis Grizzard was editor of the Atlanta Journal when Aaron chased Ruth's record. He wrote about the racist reactions in his book, "If I Ever Get Back to Georgia, I'm Gonna Nail My Feet to the Ground."

"The more we wrote about Aaron's challenge, the more phone calls we got calling us (racial slur) lovers," Grizzard wrote. "The callers all wanted to point out that Aaron might ... break the record, but that he had more at-bats than Ruth."

Those callers were singing the same tune as my old schoolmate. When Black people achieve greatness, some find a reason to diminish it.

In a 2014 interview with USA Today, Aaron said he still kept the racist letters sent to him when he was close to the home run mark. He said he did so to "remind myself that we are not that far removed from when I was chasing the record.

"A lot of things have happened in this country, but we have so far to go," Aaron told the newspaper. "There's not a whole lot that has changed. ... Sure, this country has a Black president, but when you look at a Black president, President Obama is left with his foot stuck in the mud from all of the Republicans with the way he's treated.

"We have moved in the right direction, and there have been improvements, but we still have a long ways to go. The bigger difference is back then they had hoods. Now they have neckties and starched shirts."

USA Today reported that the Braves were "besieged by hundreds of letters, emails and phone calls deriding Aaron" for his comments. In 1974 Aaron was the target of hatred because he was a Black man with the audacity to break Ruth's record. In 2014 it was because had the nerve to speak out in defense of the Black president.

Aaron cited Jackie Robinson as his inspiration. In a contribution to a 1999 Time magazine special section on Robinson, Aaron wrote that he was in awe of Robinson when the ballplayer came to his hometown of Mobile when Aaron was 14 years old. Robinson "changed my life" by breaking baseball's color barrier, Aaron wrote, and was the only person who was truly "bigger than life."

Robinson and Aaron were great ballplayers who carried the twin burdens. They were targets of abuse and discrimination and also expected to use their fame to advocate for the human rights of Black people.

"To be honest, I feel somewhat guilty that I didn't do possibly as much as I could have done," Aaron said at the 2018 "Hank Aaron Champion for Justice Awards" hosted by the National Center for Civil and Human Rights in downtown Atlanta. "But (Andrew Young) told me, 'Don't feel that (way) because what you were doing on your end was much (bigger) than what we were doing on our end.' So he makes me feel a little better."

Aaron said then that he supported athletes speaking out against social injustice. At the time, players from several championship teams had declined the traditional visit to the White House because of Donald Trump's bigoted words and actions. Aaron said he understood their stance and that he probably also would decline to go, adding "there's nobody there I want to see."

Aaron angered racists in 1974 because they didn't want a Black man to break Ruth's record. Doing so helped Aaron make a case as the greatest ballplayer of all time. His 143.1 bWAR ranks seventh of all time, but

Boxing great Muhammad Ali (left) talks with Hank Aaron during a January 2001 ceremony where President Bill Clinton presented Aaron, Ali and others with the Presidential Citizens Medal. The medal was established by President Richard Nixon in 1969 to recognize exemplary service by any citizen. (AP Photo)

I put unofficial asterisks next to the numbers of nearly all the players listed above Aaron.

Ruth's 182.5 WAR is best by a wide margin. But Ruth and other greats excelled during an era when not all the best ballplayers were in the majors because Black players were barred (a small number of Latinos played before Robinson). The rules protected Ruth from truly open competition, a fact that's hardly mentioned when Ruth is declared the greatest ballplayer ever.

Barry Bonds is No. 4 in career WAR, the highest among players who played post-integration. He broke Aaron's home run record in 2007 and finished with 762, a record that stands. The argument against Bonds as best of all time is the same one that's kept him out of the Hall of Fame: his use of performance-enhancing drugs.

Aaron didn't dispute Bonds' record. He congratulated Bonds in a video message played in the stadium after he hit No. 756. But Aaron once said that if Bonds and other confirmed PED users from the steroids era were admitted to the Hall, it should be with an asterisk next to their names.

Exclude pre-integration players and Bonds, and Mays (156.2) is the career WAR leader with Aaron just behind. Mays was the superior outfielder. Aaron had more hits (3,771 vs. 3,283). He's still the career leader in RBIs (2,297) and total bases (6,856).

Aaron is a hero to many Americans, especially Black people. He's among the best ballplayers who ever lived and supplanted Babe Ruth as Home Run King. There's nothing my old classmate or anyone else can do to change that. ◗

Hank Aaron points to the large crowd gathered in a Harlem park on June 18, 1974 during New York City's Hank Aaron Day celebration. The salute to Aaron included a procession and a ceremony at City Hall. (AP Photo)

'HE ALWAYS ANSWERED THE CALL'

Aaron Used His Legendary Status to Help Others

By Jennifer Brett, Shelia Poole and Eric Stirgus | January 22, 2021

The ballroom at the Atlanta Marriott Marquis was packed the night Hank Aaron celebrated his 75th birthday. Former President Bill Clinton was there, as were former Gov. Roy Barnes, former Atlanta Mayors Andrew Young and Shirley Franklin and former Braves owner Ted Turner.

"Hank has been the perfect role model for me, on the field and off the field," Braves player turned commentator Brian Jordan said that night in February 2009. "This is the guy I wanted to be."

While Aaron was the star of the show, the event was in fact about helping others. The celebration that drew a capacity crowd of sports, business and political leaders benefited Aaron's Chasing the Dream Foundation, known for providing 44 grants each year to the Boys & Girls Clubs of America.

"It's wonderful to see him in the second half of his life working with young people to give them opportunities that, quite frankly, he didn't have," Franklin said of the Braves' beloved No. 44 that night.

It's the kind of story those in Atlanta's philanthropic circles love to share. Long after his jersey was retired, Hammerin' Hank was still swinging for the fences in the name of charity.

"Hank Aaron was more than just the home run king," said Tommy Dortch, who served as chairman of 100 Black Men of Atlanta before becoming chairman of 100 Black Men of America. "He was a phenomenal humanitarian. He was a civil rights leader and he always fought for the rights of others. In addition to that, he was committed to seeing young people succeed by having their dreams and helping them to become reality."

Berry College President Steve Briggs was among the many leaders mourning Aaron in a spirit of gratitude.

"We are grateful to his Chasing the Dream Foundation, which in partnership with Berry College supporters, provides scholarships to deserving students, who might not otherwise be able to experience Berry's distinctive education," Briggs said. "Like Martha Berry, Hank and Billye Aaron brought to life a vision for helping children and young people achieve their dreams."

The Aarons invested more than $2 million over the years in endowments and scholarships to Atlanta Technical College, which officials there say has resulted in an economic impact of about $10 million to the school. Through the couple, the college has eight endowed scholarships of $1,000 to $1,500 each semester along with funding up to $600 each to 12 to 20 students per semester who need a little help paying their tuition.

The couple hosted events at their southwest Atlanta home where culinary students honed their skills. In many ways, Aaron saw himself in the students, many of whom grew up in neighborhoods nearby.

"He always said he was trying to give back to his community and people who look like him," said the college's president, Victoria Seals.

A model of generosity on and off the field, Hank Aaron signs a baseball for a fan before a 1974 game. (AP Photo)

The college renamed its academic complex after Hank Aaron as part of an 86th birthday party celebration for the legend.

The Aarons' philanthropic efforts over the years have also benefited institutions such as the Morehouse School of Medicine and the UNCF Mayor's Masked Ball Atlanta.

Over the years, the couple donated $4.2 million to the Atlanta-based medical school, said Bennie L. Harris, senior vice president for the Office of Institutional Advancement for the Morehouse School of Medicine.

That included $3 million donated to Morehouse School of Medicine as part of an expansion of academic facilities at the Atlanta institution. The gift helped fund an expansion of the Hugh Gloster Medical Education building and created the Billye Suber Aaron Student Pavilion, which opened in 2017.

"Aaron believed very strongly in the importance of giving back and was particularly interested in helping students from Mobile, where he grew up," said Harris, who said the legend was particularly interested in the issue of health care.

During their conversations, Aaron talked about "how blessed he had been to achieve the things he had achieved and felt a responsibility to give back."

To the world, Aaron was a "baseball giant," Harris said in a statement. "To Morehouse School of Medicine, he was also a wonderful advocate, philanthropist, businessman and friend. "

"He was the epitome of grace and generosity. A true icon," said Jack Sawyer, partner and managing director at Cresset Capital Management, a past honorary co-chair of the Mayor's Masked Ball. "Hank and Billye were imbued with a commitment to service of others. Hank was, of course, fiercely competitive on the field. Off the field, he had a reputation for caring and doing for others."

Legendary Events owner Tony Conway shared happy memories of Aaron from events through the years.

"We were honored to be a part of The Hank Aaron Foundation Gala at the Delta Flight Museum; I loved hearing Mr. Aaron speak about his passion for the kids," said Conway. "I was equally honored when producing The Tyler Perry Studios' Grand Opening for 850 guests and hearing that Mr. Aaron would be accompanied by his grandson. It was so great seeing him and Mrs. Aaron again and meeting their grandson."

Longtime public relations pro Bob Hope was also involved with the foundation's benefit at the flight museum.

"Hank and Billye are literally the most giving people I ever met," he said. "Their dedication to their scholarship program to give youngsters a chance to pursue their talents was very pure and honest."

Former Mayor and former U.N. Ambassador Young said in an interview that Aaron probably helped more than 2,000 young people through various philanthropic efforts.

"He probably gave more money away since his baseball days helping young people continue their dreams, develop their dreams than the money he made in baseball," Young said.

Sometimes, Aaron's efforts on behalf of youths took on a fun and casual tone.

"He came on air with me and I brought in a Black youth baseball team. They were about 8 years old," recalled longtime Atlanta broadcaster Frank Ski. "He spent so much quality time with them talking about everything. It was very special."

Glenda Hatchett, the founder of The Hatchett Firm, admired Aaron as a dedicated civic supporter over the years. The two headlined the Atlanta Bar Association's "Celebrating Service" luncheon, held at The Temple in October 2008.

"I called upon Mr. Aaron numerous times to support our efforts to rehabilitate and inspire our children. He always answered the call," said Hatchett, who starred in television shows "Judge Hatchett" and "The Verdict With Judge Hatchett." "I thank Mr. Aaron for his tremendous work and generosity to the Boys and Girls Clubs of America during my tenure as a national board member. What a miraculous hero on and off the field. His work and commitment to young people will live on for generations to come." ●

Hank Aaron waves to the crowd during a 2015 pre-game ceremony celebrating the 50th Braves baseball season in Atlanta. (AP Photo)

A TEAMMATE AND FRIEND

Ralph Garr: Hank Aaron 'Did So Much for Me'

By Tim Tucker | January 25, 2021

Ralph Garr, Hank Aaron's teammate for seven seasons and his friend for more than 50 years, thanks Aaron for many things.

The long list includes the National League batting title that Garr won with the Braves in 1974, the year Aaron broke Babe Ruth's career home run record.

"Give him credit for me winning the batting title," Garr said Monday. "(Pitchers) were thinking about him and weren't paying any attention to me."

Garr was the runner on second base when Aaron tied Ruth with home run No. 714 on April 4, 1974, in Cincinnati. He was in the dugout when Aaron hit No. 715 four days later in Atlanta, ending the chase of Ruth.

"Hank said (before that game), 'I'm going to try to get it over with, fellas, as soon as I can, so we can go on and just play baseball,'" Garr recalled.

Even as the pursuit of the record consumed the sports world, Aaron prioritized winning games.

"That was his intention every time he hit the ballpark," Garr said. "He was going to do everything he could to help his team win."

In the more than four decades since that historic home run, Garr remained in frequent contact with Aaron. He was shocked to learn of Aaron's death when he got a phone call from one of Aaron's sons. Garr, who lives in Houston, had last spoken with Aaron just a week earlier.

"Hank Aaron was a great baseball player, but he was an even better human being," Garr, now 75, said. "If you notice, he never did talk bitter toward anybody. Now, I think he had a right to say some things, but he never did talk negative about anybody that ever played before or after him. He has always been a guy who was positive about everything. That's what he taught (former teammate) Dusty (Baker) and me: If you can't help somebody, don't hurt nobody.

"That's what I love about him: He just made all of us care about one another. He didn't care what color you were. All of us were human beings, and we should love and respect one another at all times.

"I used to room with Hank Aaron sometimes ... when we'd go on the road in spring training. He did so much for me and Dusty and everybody that we just want the world to know what a wonderful man he was, other than being a remarkable baseball player."

Garr was drafted by the Braves in 1967 and made his MLB debut in September 1968. The speedy outfielder split the 1969 and 1970 seasons between Atlanta and the minor leagues, became a big-league regular in 1971 and played for the Braves through 1975. His .353 batting average, 214 hits and 17 triples led the National League in 1974. Hitting leadoff or second in the batting order, he averaged 29 stolen bases a year

Hank Aaron speaks at a press conference at Atlanta-Fulton County Stadium in 1982. (Nancy Mangiafico/The Atlanta Journal-Constitution)

from 1971 through 1974 – and could have had more steals if not for the slugger hitting behind him.

"I came up (nicknamed) as the 'Road Runner,' and the Braves advertised that for a while," Garr said. "But when Mr. Aaron was batting third, you didn't need (a lot of stolen bases) because he could drive you in from first base pretty good, too."

The Braves traded Garr in December 1975, and he played five more seasons with the Chicago White Sox and California Angels. He had a career batting average of .306.

Garr is now in his 37th year as a scout for the Braves, a career that started because Aaron invited his friend to visit him at the baseball winter meetings in Houston in 1984. During that visit, Garr expressed interest in working for the Braves. Aaron, then the team's director of player development, and Paul Snyder, then the director of scouting, hired Garr as a scout and minor-league baserunning coach.

"I have enjoyed every minute of it," Garr said. "I was able to watch (Tom) Glavine and (John) Smoltz and Chipper Jones and Andruw Jones and all those wonderful ballplayers come up through the Braves organization. It has been a wonderful experience for me and my family.

"It all started because Hank Aaron called me and I went down there to the winter meetings as a friend and ended up being hired."

From his early playing days through his long scouting career, Garr relied upon Aaron's advice.

"He wasn't a guy who made a whole lot of noise and everything and said a whole lot," Garr said, "but if you ever went to him for advice, he would really take pride in giving you the best advice he thought possible for that situation."

When they were teammates as players, "he would always tell me that you've got to be true to yourself and work on your weakness some, but stay with your strength and work hard every day and do what you know is right and play the game hard," Garr said. "And (his) No. 1 thing was: Be a good teammate, and respect the game of baseball." ●

A former teammate and longtime friend of Hank Aaron, Ralph Garr spoke of Aaron's generosity and integrity following the legend's passing. (The Atlanta Journal-Constitution)

Hank Aaron is carried off by elated teammates after crossing home plate for his 715th career home run at Atlanta Stadium. (AP Photo)

714

Aaron Ties Ruth in Cincinnati

By Jesse Outlar | April 5, 1974

In his first swing of the 1974 baseball season, Henry Aaron, a living legend, caught up with the ghost of Babe Ruth in the home run race that started 21 years ago.

The incomparable Aaron resolved the controversy of what he was supposed to do in Cincinnati by driving a Jack Billingham pitch over the left wall in the first inning Thursday for historic No. 714. Now, Aaron needs only one more to become the most productive home run hitter of all time.

When the sun-soaked afternoon at Riverfront Stadium ended, however, Aaron wasn't as excited as the 52,154 fans, including Vice President Gerald Ford, who witnessed the memorable event.

"I've thought so much about it," said Aaron, holding the home run ball in his left hand and a mike in his right. "Now it's just another homer after we lost the game. If we had won, I'd be in the other room drinking champagne. But we lost."

Aaron was also disturbed that the Cincinnati front office had declined his request for a moment of silence in memory of Dr. Martin Luther King Jr. on the anniversary of the death of the famed civil rights leader in Memphis.

"Rev. Jesse Jackson had asked me to make the request," said Aaron, "and I thought they should have done it. But my request was turned down."

Aaron's 714th home run was just one of several career milestones which have occurred in Cincinnati.

It was here that Aaron played his first major league game 21 seasons ago in Crosley Field. It was here that he collected his 3,000th hit.

After a simmering debate as to whether Aaron would swing for No. 714 in the opening series, Commissioner Bowie Kuhn ordered the Braves to play Aaron.

Aaron quickly proved that Kuhn is a better manager than commissioner. The long suspense surrounding the greatest record in sports lasted just long enough for Aaron to come to bat. With Ralph Garr on second, Mike Lum on first and one out, Aaron strolled to the plate. He did not swing officially until Billingham worked the count to 3-1. When Billingham came in with a fastball that didn't sink, Aaron blasted it to the left of the 375 mark in left field.

Aaron also brought the crowd and the Braves to their feet in the fifth when he walked and scored from first on a two-base error.

After finishing the 1973 season with 713 home runs, Hank Aaron wasted no time when spring rolled around, hitting his 714th on opening day of 1974 to tie Babe Ruth's longstanding record. (AP Photo)

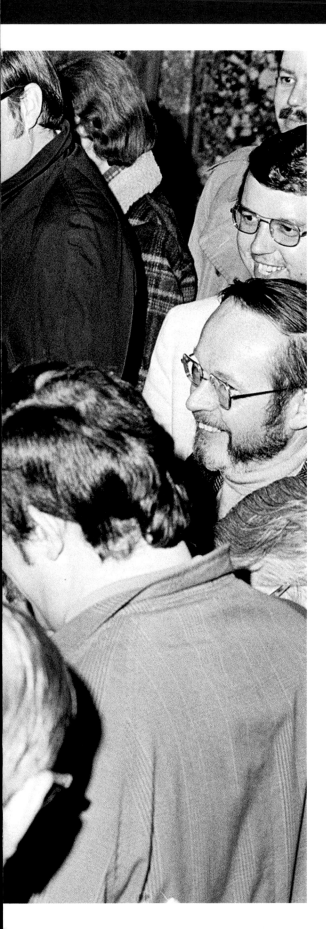

"I know I can hit home runs," said Aaron, smiling, "but I wanted to see if I could still score all the way from first."

Aaron's 714th home run occurred on his 11,289th major league at bat, compared to 8,399 for Ruth – 2,890 fewer.

But the difference in at-bats did not lessen the magic of the moment. Aaron, in his customary cleanup position as the fourth hitter in the Braves batting order, appeared after Ralph Garr had walked, Mike Lum had lined a single to left and Darrell Evans had flied out to left field.

Billingham, a 19-game winner for the Reds last season, was low on his first pitch, then missed the plate with a slow curve for ball two. Aaron took a fastball for a strike, but the count went to three balls and one strike on a low outside sinker.

"The ball was slippery," Billingham said later. "On the next pitch, I threw a sinker but it just didn't sink. It was going toward the outside part of the plate and it tailed in. It was my mistake. But that's what makes Hank Aaron great. He hits mistakes."

Aaron swung his white ash, 34-ounce, 33½-inch bat and the ball rose in a low trajectory, similar to that of a properly struck 2-iron shot in golf. The ball disappeared behind the 12-foot fence slightly to the left of the 375-foot sign in left-center field.

But the homer didn't give him the anticipated thrill.

"It doesn't matter what homer it is," said Aaron, "and I mean this. It's no fun when you lose."

Unfortunately the most memorable day of Atlanta Braves history had a typical ending, the Braves lost 7-6 in 11 innings. But it was a day that will be remembered as long as the game of baseball is played.

As Aaron left the crowded room near the clubhouse, he was swarmed by autograph-seekers. One man had a baseball autographed by Babe Ruth. Aaron added his signature. Their names belong on the same ball. ◗

Hank Aaron tells reporters about a telephone call he received from President Richard M. Nixon congratulating him for tying Babe Ruth's all-time home run record of 714. The 40-year-old slugger said, "He just congratulated me and wished me well and hoped I could hit 715 in a hurry." (AP Photo)

THE ATLANTA CONSTITUTION
For 105 Years the South's Standard Newspaper

VOL. 106, No. 247 ★★ P. O. Box 4689 ATLANTA, GA. 30302, FRIDAY, APRIL 5, 1974 120 PAGES, 6 SECTIONS ★★★★ TEN CENTS

Aaron Hits 714

By JESSE OUTLAR
Constitution Sports Editor

With the First Swing of 1974 Season Hank Aaron Tied Legendary Record

Babe Ruth Held Record 39 Years

Mrs. Ruth
'I Wish Him Luck'

No. 714: Slightly to the Left of the 375 Sign

On Deck
What About No. 715?

By WAYNE MINSHEW

13 Georgia Counties Due Disaster Relief

By SAM HOPKINS and JEFF NESMITH

Neighbors Scour Wreckage of Resaca Home in Which Four Members of Goebel Family Were Killed

See TORNADOES, Page 20-A

Washington Now Acupuncture Hub

SHIRLEY PATTERSON STANDS IN RUBBLE OF HER HOUSE TRAILER
Scene in Pineville Community Five Miles West of Berea

Allen Likely to Appeal Theft Ring Conviction

— Aaron —
From Page 1-A

— Home Run —
From Page 1-A

— Tornadoes —
From Page 1-A

The Atlanta Journal
"COVERS DIXIE LIKE THE DEW"

FINAL HOME EDITION

Vol. 92, No. 95 P.O. Box 4689 Atlanta, Ga. 30302, Friday Evening, April 5, 1974 102 Pages—6 Sections ★★ Price 10 Cents

Twister-Ravaged N. Georgians Count Dead, Begin Rebuilding

WALLOPS 714

Hank Catches Ghost of Ruth

By FRANK HYLAND

16 Killed, $15 Million In Damages

Nixon Calls Aaron To Congratulate Him

WASHINGTON (AP)

SECURITY GUARD CAUGHT THE HOME RUN BALL
Clarence Williams With Aaron (Page 6D)

INSIDE TODAY
Fears Surface Patty Is Dead

HANK'S FANS
Continued from Page 1A

Aaron New King Of the Mountain

Continued from Page 1A

Senate Calls Aaron 'Legendary Figure'

DEADLINE
Continued from Page 1A

TWISTERS
Continued from Page 1A

Former Official Free for Appeal

'NAUGHTY BOYS...'
LONDON (UPI)

THE ATLANTA CONSTITUTION

For 105 Years the South's Standard Newspaper

VOL. 106, No. 250 ★★★   P. O. Box 4689   ATLANTA, GA. 30302, TUESDAY, APRIL 9, 1974   68 PAGES, 3 SECTIONS ★★★★★   TEN CENTS

Aaron Hammers No. 715 And Moves Ahead of Ruth

NEWS THIS MORNING

GOOD MORNING! Thunderstorms across the state should be ending this morning. Windy and cooler weather is expected for today. For more details, Page 2-A.

WORLD

TEL AVIV — Israeli fighter crashes in flames after the two pilots bail out over Lebanon during renewed clashes in the Golan Heights. It was Israel's first loss of a warplane since the October war. Page 34-B.

ADDIS ABABA — Ethiopia's chief of staff resigns after rebellious troops seize control of a provincial city to protest alleged corruption in the military and government, according to the official Ethiopian news agency. Page 34-B.

NATION

NEW YORK — Bank posts a record-tying 10 per cent prime interest rate, sending the stock market into a spin with prices closing at their lowest point since mid-February. Page 7-C.

SAN ANTONIO — Court-appointed attorneys for accused mass-slayer Elmer Wayne Henley tell a judge that Houston police violated their client's rights when he confessed he was involved in a series of 27 sex-torture murders. Page 34-B.

WASHINGTON — In a report to the Senate Armed Services Committee, Sen. Sam Nunn reviews his recent inspection tour of NATO countries, stressing the need for congressional attention to NATO and criticizing France for independent stances on European defense. Page 8-A.

WASHINGTON — Half of every dollar contributed to the Epilepsy Foundation of America goes for overhead and fund-raising costs, concedes the executive vice president of the foundation. Paul E. Funk says his group has trouble recruiting volunteers because prospects feel that they will be identified as having epilepsy. Page 8-A.

GEORGIA

GEORGIA, which led the South in industrial expansion during the past six years, ranked third last year. But, the head of the Department of Community Development says 1973 was one of the best years in his department's history. Page 17-A.

AT AN AFTERNOON press conference, Gov. Jimmy Carter praises Dr. Gary Miller for "unlimited courage and tenacity," but says those traits work against "the harmonious development" of mental health programs. Miller was dismissed last Friday as chief of the state's mental health program. Page 10-A.

ATLANTA

DELTA, Eastern and National airlines petition the Civil Aeronautics Board for nonstop service between Atlanta, London and Paris. Six other carriers earlier had informed the CAB of interest in the trans-Atlantic flights. Page 7-C.

WILLIAM H. WILLIAMS, charged with extorting $700,000 in the abduction of Atlanta Constitution editor Reg Murphy, undergoes a court-ordered psychiatric examination at a private hospital. Page 19-A.

Henry Aaron's home run legacy began in 1954 in St. Louis. Sports Editor Jesse Outlar was at the stadium to see home run 715 Monday. His report, along with full coverage of the historic night, begins on Page 1-C.

BY WAYNE MINSHEW

Undaunted by the swirl of controversy surrounding his quest for baseball immortality, Hank Aaron became the game's all-time home run king Monday night when he smashed his 715th of an illustrious career.

The 40-year-old Atlanta Braves superstar left behind the ghost of Babe Ruth when he connected for the historic clout in the fourth inning off lefthander Al Downing of the Los Angeles Dodgers.

It was No. 44 at the plate and No. 44 on the mound. And Aaron hammered a 1-0 pitch over the left field fence just to the right of the 385-foot marker and circled the bases for the 715th time accompanied by a massive fireworks display.

A sellout crowd of 52,870 rose as one for a standing ovation and Aaron's teammates poured out of the dugout and the bullpen to greet him.

After touching home plate, the Hammer was lifted by and carried a few steps on the shoulders of his fellow Braves, before he broke away and trotted to a special box. There he embraced wife Billye and his parents, Mr. and Mrs. Herbert Aaron of Mobile, Ala.

He stayed with his family about two minutes before returning to the field and holding aloft the historic ball.

The ball carried about 400 feet and did not get into the bleacher seats. It was brought back to Aaron by Atlanta relief pitcher Tom House.

The legendary Ruth, who died in 1948, had hit 714 home runs, the last three in 1935. He played 22 seasons and batted 8,399 times.

The soft-spoken Aaron's record shot came in the third game of his 21st season. It came on his 11,295th at-bat and in his 2,967th game.

"I just thank God it's all over," he told the cheering crowd.

Moments later, black Hall of Famer Monte Irvin, representing Commissioner Bowie Kuhn, presented Aaron with a $3,800 wrist watch, diamond-studded and with the figure 715 imprinted in gold.

Irvin was booed loudly by the crowd. The boos were aimed, however, at Kuhn, who had ordered the Braves to play Aaron in Cincinnati Sunday—against Atlanta management's wishes.

Aaron had ended his highly publicized chase of Ruth last Thursday, opening day in Cincinnati, with his first swing of the season. He propelled a three-run homer off Jack Billingham to tie Ruth at 714.

Henry Louis Aaron grew up as a quiet, shy boy in Mobile, Ala., where he was raised by adoring parents. He is still a soft-spoken man and as such, could hardly be more unlike the legend whose place he takes at the top of the home run list.

Ruth was one of the most colorful, charismatic athletes ever and in both his life and his career, he went from one emotional extreme to another.

In 1902, for example, the courts of Maryland rules seven-year-old George Herman Ruth "a hopeless incorrigible" and placed him in a home for wayward boys, where he found guidance and learned the game of baseball.

Forty-six years later that "hopeless incorrigible" stood before stands packed with cheering, weeping fans who came to the "House that Ruth Built" to view the great Bambino wear a Yankee uniform for the last time.

In the interim the Babe belted long, majestic homers and by the time he finished in 1935 — ironically wearing a Braves' uni-

See HOMER, Page 18-A

Hank Aaron's Swing for the Record: 715 Goo...

HOME RUN FRENZY

'Yowie! Yowie! Y...

Aaron and Parents: 'Glad It's Over'

Nixon Signs Minimum Wage Hike

WASHINGTON (UPI) — President Nixon signed legislation Monday raising the minimum wage in three steps from the current $1.60 to $2.30 an hour and extending its coverage to domestic servants and governmental employes.

It will be raised to $2 an hour May 1, to $2.10 an hour Jan. 1, 1975, and to $2.30 an hour Jan. 1, 1976.

Approving a bill almost identical to one he vetoed only seven months ago, Nixon included in minimum wage coverage for the first time domestic service employes, with the exception of baby sitters and paid companions, all state and local government workers and to retail service workers employed by chain stores.

All told, between 7 and 8 million workers never before covered now will be, bringing 54 million Americans under the minimum wage law.

The law also will extend provisions requiring payment of overtime in excess of 40 hours a week to 8 million workers not covered —mostly in hotels, restaurants, nursing homes, bowling alleys and similar businesses.

It will also extend overtime provisions to policemen and firemen, but under a different formula.

The measure had passed the House and Senate by large majorities and although the administration was not entirely satisfied with it, there appeared little chance of congressional opponents sustaining a presidential veto.

Nixon skipped an elaborate signing ceremony and the only ones present for the historic presidential signature were Labor Secretary Peter Brennan and Nixon's assistant, Kenneth Cole.

The President removed one pen from a box

and signed the bill. He slid the pen across the desk to Brennan, picked the bill up in his right hand and tossed it into an out box on the corner of his desk.

In a prepared statement, Nixon said, "On the whole, this legislation is more good than bad and I have concluded that the best interests of the American people will be served by signing it into law."

The administration had argued that the bill would result in many teen-agers losing their jobs because employers would let them go rather than pay the extra money.

And in his statement, Nixon said he thought acceptable minimum wage law also should contain a special youth differential, adding "although $247 does change the tests for special

minimum wage certificates for part-time work by full-time students and permits pilot programs in selected areas for out-of-school youth, I regret that the Congress did not go as far as I wished in protecting both training and work opportunities for the youth."

"Although I have some reservations about portions of this legislation, its basic purpose—to increase the minimum wage for working men and women of this country—deserves the support of all Americans," Nixon said.

"The federally legislated minimum wage for most American workers has remained static for six years, despite a number of increases in the cost of living, raising the minimum wage is now a matter of justice that can no longer be fairly delayed."

'BREAKING IT WILL BE SOMETHING ELSE'

Aaron Looks Ahead to 715

By Wayne Minshew | April 5, 1974

"Tying the record is great, but breaking it will be something else," said Henry Aaron after hitting the 714th home run of his career in the season opener against the Cincinnati Reds.

"Next, I may run around the bases backwards," Aaron added. "This was just another home run – it lost a little of the edge when we lost the game."

With No. 714, the Braves' slugger moved to within one swing of becoming baseball's all-time home run leader.

The question is: Will Atlanta fans get a chance to see No. 715 clobbered into sports history in their home ballpark?

Should Aaron fail to connect in the next game against the Reds, his next opportunity would come in Atlanta-Fulton County Stadium, when the Braves open their home season against the Los Angeles Dodgers.

Aaron's wife Billye, who says she hasn't noticed any signs of tension in the right-handed slugger, hopes 715 comes in Atlanta. "Oh sure, you like to see home runs at home because you have a warm feeling for home, but you have to consider the fates. You can't be too choosy and pick the sites for anything. As I said, the fates have more to do with it.

"I am happy that he hit 714 because it had to come somewhere. And if No. 715 comes in Atlanta, that much better."

"Now or later it's good to see Henry break Ruth's record," said Aaron's father, Herbert. "Perhaps it would have been better in Atlanta, but you take what you can get. I'm happy for Henry."

Braves officials expressed delight, too. "It's hard to describe how I feel," said president Bill Bartholomay, "… we might win the pennant."

Aaron said Thursday, after delivering the blow to tie Babe Ruth, that he plans to play Saturday in Cincinnati. And he will be trying his best.

"Certainly, I'll play the game the way it is supposed to be played," Aaron said. "If I get a pitch to hit out, I'll certainly try to dispose of it."

Cincinnati's starting pitcher will be lefthander Don Gullett, who has given up more homers – seven – to the Atlanta star than anyone else on the Reds staff.

Saturday's game is an afternoon contest, starting at 2:30 p.m.

The finale of the three-game series will be played Sunday afternoon – and Aaron doesn't plan to be in the lineup. "Here again, I feel I still owe the fans of Atlanta something," he said. "I think they deserve a shot at seeing 715."

Thus, while Aaron will play Saturday, and play his best, it won't bother him too much if he fails to tag No. 715. ◗

Hank Aaron greets his wife, Billye, and his father, Herbert, after tying Babe Ruth's home run record at Riverfront Stadium in Cincinnati. (AP Photo)

715

Aaron Hammers No. 715 And Moves Ahead of Ruth

By Wayne Minshew | April 9, 1974

Undaunted by the swirl of controversy surrounding his quest for baseball immortality, Hank Aaron became the game's all-time home run king when he smashed his 715th of an illustrious career.

The 40-year-old Atlanta Braves superstar left behind the ghost of Babe Ruth when he connected for the historic clout in the fourth inning off lefthander Al Downing of the Los Angeles Dodgers.

It was No. 44 at the plate and No. 44 on the mound. And Aaron hammered a 1-0 pitch over the left field fence just to the right of the 385-foot marker and circled the bases for the 715th time accompanied by a massive fireworks display.

A sellout crowd of 53,775 rose as one for a standing ovation and Aaron's teammates poured out of the dugout and the bullpen to greet him.

After touching home plate, the Hammer was lifted by and carried a few steps on the shoulders of his fellow Braves before he broke away and trotted to a special box. There he embraced wife Billye and his parents, Mr. and Mrs. Herbert Aaron of Mobile, Alabama.

He stayed with his family about two minutes before returning to the field and holding aloft the historic ball.

The ball carried about 400 feet and did not get into the bleacher seats. It was brought back to Aaron by Atlanta relief pitcher Tom House.

The legendary Ruth, who died in 1948, had hit 714 home runs, the last three in 1935. He played 22 seasons and batted 8,399 times.

The soft-spoken Aaron's record shot came in the third game of his 21st season. It came on his 11,295th at-bat and in his 2,967th game.

"I just thank God it's all over," he told the cheering crowd.

Moments later, Black Hall of Famer Monte Irvin, representing Commissioner Bowie Kuhn, presented Aaron with a $3,000 wrist watch, diamond-studded and with the figure 715 imprinted in gold.

Irvin was booed loudly by the crowd. The boos were aimed, however, at Kuhn, who had ordered the Braves to play Aaron in Cincinnati Sunday – against Atlanta management's wishes.

Aaron had ended his highly publicized chase of Ruth last Thursday, opening day in Cincinnati, with his first swing of the season. He propelled a three-run homer off Jack Billingham to tie Ruth at 714.

Henry Louis Aaron grew up as a quiet, shy boy in Mobile, Alabama, where he was raised by adoring parents. He is still a soft-spoken man and, as such, could

Hank Aaron hits his 715th home run in front of a sellout crowd in Atlanta on April 8, 1974. (File Photo/The Atlanta Journal-Constitution)

hardly be more unlike the legend whose place he takes at the top of the home run list.

Ruth was one of the most colorful, charismatic athletes ever, and in both his life and his career, he went from one emotional extreme to another.

In 1902, for example, the courts of Maryland ruled 7-year-old George Herman Ruth "a hopeless Incorrigible" and placed him in a home for wayward boys, where he found guidance and learned the game of baseball.

Forty-six years later that "hopeless Incorrigible" stood before stands packed with cheering, weeping fans who came to the "House that Ruth Built" to view the great Bambino wear a Yankee uniform for the last time.

In the interim, the Babe belted long, majestic homers and by the time he finished in 1935 – ironically wearing a (Boston) Braves uniform – he had accumulated that famous total of 714.

Aaron, who began his career as a skinny rookie in 1954, hit only 13 homers that first season, but by the time the Braves moved South in 1966, he had reached 389. He found a home in Atlanta Stadium, dubbed the Launching Pad, and homers flew off his potent bat.

When he hit his 600th round tripper off Gaylord Perry of San Francisco, the names Ruth and Aaron began to come in the same breath when people talked baseball. And for the past season and a half, not a day has gone by without someone mentioning the Babe's name to Aaron.

Aaron and Ruth were as unlike on the field as off. The Babe, a lefthander, had a majestic, sweeping stroke while Hammerin' Hank, who once batted cross-handed, got the job done with quick, strong wrists and a downward swing.

Until Ruth came along, swinging from the end of a dreaded 42-ounce weapon, the game's great hitters had choked up on the bat and punched out their singles and doubles; they went for average, not for the fences.

But Ruth proved that homers are "box office" and Aaron has followed in his footsteps, writing a home run story the baseball-loving public will repeat as long as the game is played.

Ruth's home runs changed the game, as players and fans alike fell in love with raw power. The Bambino could do wrong, although he reportedly ate eye-popping meals prior to games and drank enough beer to wash it down. His night life was unmatched, for he reputedly knew no curfew.

Still, Ruth, who broke in as a pitcher in 1914 and compiled an 87-44 record before moving to the outfield on a permanent basis, swung the bat as few men ever have. He averaged .343 for his career and in 1927 he struck 60 homers, a one-season record which stood until 1961, when a controversial young outfielder named Roger Maris totaled 61 for the Yankees.

Pennants flew over Yankee Stadium almost yearly because of Ruth and the rest of the club's so-called Murderer's Row. He became a living legend because of his lifestyle and the way he played ball. But he also loved kids and would sign autographs for them for hours on end.

Babe Ruth had a love affair going with baseball until 1934 when, according to his widow, in the book "The Babe and I," the Yankees hurt him deeply by not hiring him as their manager after he apparently had reached the end of his playing career.

So, Ruth went with the Boston Braves and on May 25, 1935, hit three homers in one game at Pittsburgh. They were the 712th, 713th and 714th of his career. He was not to hit another and called in reporters on June 2 to tell them his baseball playing career was over. ●

Hank Aaron shows off his home run ball, caught and returned by Braves reliever Tom House. (File Photo/The Atlanta Journal-Constitution)

★ ★ ★
ELECTRIC ATMOSPHERE

Yowie! Yowie! Yowie!

By Jeff Nesmith | April 9, 1974

It was the nearest thing to World Series excitement Atlanta Stadium has seen.

The stadium had erupted Monday night with a volcanic emotion that perhaps was best articulated by a lady in a red suit who stood at the Aisle 207 sign, jumped up and down and hollered again and again, "Yowie! Yowie! Yowie!"

Hank Aaron, who earlier confided that he spent the afternoon of the big day watching soap operas on television, had hit his 715th career home run. That and the attendant fireworks, balloons and tributes goaded 53,775 baseball fans into a screaming frenzy.

Then, even before an official tally of the night's attendance had been computed, many of those fans had gone.

It was a cold and windy night and they had seen what they came to see. By Aaron's next time at bat – to ground out and receive a standing ovation even for that – the empty blue seats in the outfield made it look like an ordinary night at Atlanta Stadium.

"He does what his momma tells him and I told him to go out there tonight and hit," Mrs. Herbert Aaron of Mobile, Alabama, said before the game. "He's going to hit it tonight."

Mrs. Aaron and her husband, along with Hank Aaron's wife, Billye, and other members of his immediate family sat in a field level box, entertained prior to the game by the easy jokes of entertainer Pearl Bailey.

"I knew he was going to hit that other one in Cincinnati, too," Mrs. Aaron continued, "but I wasn't there for that one. I couldn't stand the pressure."

"You can see a little bit of America out here tonight," Ms. Bailey offered as the baseball scent of hotdogs and popcorn built in the pre-game air. "There's happiness out here and something going on and people are saying, 'Yeah, this is where it's at.'"

When a Braves official came to escort Ms. Bailey to the microphone where she was to sing the National Anthem, she turned back to Aaron's family: "I just hope I remember the words…"

They laughed uproariously and answered questions from newsmen with what seems to be an Aaron family trait, a soft-spoken unwillingness to launch into long statements about anything.

Hank Aaron's mother, Estella, had an intuitive feeling before the Braves' April 8 game that her son would break the home run record that night. She was in attendance for the historic swing with Aaron's wife, father, and other family members. (File Photo/The Atlanta-Journal Constitution)

Yes, Mrs. Aaron was proud of her son. Yes, she was excited. Yes, she had pushed him when he was a youngster.

"But I didn't have to push him too hard, because he always did love to play baseball."

Aaron's father was asked if he enjoyed coming to Atlanta to watch his son play ball.

"I don't find it too bad," he smiled in a way that seemed to say he wouldn't be anywhere else.

And the quietest man on that side of Atlanta was Hank Aaron.

He turned away pre-game interviews. "We're going to be mighty busy tonight," he explained.

He joked quietly with other players and took his turn at batting practice as if he didn't know that scores of sportswriters from throughout the country followed his every movement en masse.

The only time he seemed even aware of the near pandemonium that surrounded him before the game was an incredulous stare he gave a youngster who broke onto the field with a program to be autographed and shouted, "Hey, Hank Aaron, C'mere."

A little over an hour later the whole build-up of promotion and excitement had ripened with Aaron's 4th inning home run.

With the smoke of the fireworks still hanging in the air and the Dodger infield still trying to calm its despondent pitcher, Aaron stood at a microphone and told the most excited stadium crowd in Atlanta's history, "I just thank God that it's over."

Several hundred feet away, the lady in the red suit was still shouting. "Yowie! Yowie! Yowie!" ●

Atlanta Stadium erupted with cheers, screams, fireworks and balloons as Hank Aaron surpassed Babe Ruth's home run record. (AP Photo)

★ ★ ★

'THE ULTIMATE THRILL'

Braves Family Overwhelmed by 715

By Charlie Roberts | April 9, 1974

There it went. There it went, Hank Aaron's 715th home run, eclipsing Babe Ruth's hallowed all-time 714. There it went, where it should have been hit like No. 500, 600 and 700 – in Atlanta Stadium – for the fans of the Southeast to treasure.

And the man said, "This has been my greatest experience in baseball, and I've had many through all the years."

The man beamed, awed by the momentous occasion and mused, "It's just the most significant accomplishment I will ever be a part of."

No, Henry Louis Aaron wasn't talking. It was two other fellows. "Man" in paragraph three was Bill Bartholomay, Braves' Chairman of the Board. In paragraph two, it was Donald Davidson, assistant to the Board Chairman. Davidson has seen Aaron hit more homers than anyone except Aaron.

"What a thrilling moment for me this is; Hank and I have been so close," said Davidson Monday, who has been connected with the Braves since Casey Stengel managed them in Boston. "I've missed seeing only four of his homers, including two because of illness in 1973. I missed another in 1971 because I was in Kansas City representing the Braves at the winter meetings.

"The most significant one he hit until now – and I'm proud of having been the guy to nickname him Hammerin' Hank way back there – was that one off Billy Muffett of St. Louis in Milwaukee in 1957. It won an 11-inning game and clinched the pennant."

Bartholomay, flushed with excitement, said, "As fan and club owner, this is the greatest moment of all. I'm fortunate to be involved. And it's much more than just baseball. It's a happy event in a country that needs good news.

"Hank has broken the one record everyone felt could never be approached, and it's wonderful for the game. It's a really fine human interest story, and it's good for it to happen to a fellow like Henry Aaron, who is warm – a great human being."

Brash Davidson's sentiment was showing through, too, and he said, "I've been involved in baseball since the 1930s, and this is the ultimate thrill. And I'll never forget what a fantastic year he had last season, a season that caused all else to be dimmed by his race to catch Ruth. At age 39 he hit .301, hit 40 homers, batted in 99 runs and scored 84. That was the year that made it possible.

"I've seen most of Hank's spring training homers, too – and don't forget he has 15 more that don't count

Braves President Bill Bartholomay presented Hank Aaron with a trophy to commemorate his 500th career home run in 1968. Years later, after Aaron hit No. 715, Bartholomay described the achievement as "the most significant accomplishment I will ever be a part of." (AP Photo)

in the 715, two in All-Star Games, three in World Series, three in championship series, six in games that were rained out and one umpire Chris Pelekoudas took away from him for allegedly stepping out of the batter's box when he hit it. That was in 1964 at Busch Stadium – hit it on the right-field roof off Curt Simmons.

"Darrell Evans, for one, lost some publicity last year because of Hank's fantastic year, but Hank deserves all he's getting. He's a great person," said Davidson. "And, Evans could get it back some year when he breaks Roger Maris' record of 61 homers. He has the ability to do it."

Potter Palmer and Tom Reynolds, two directors of the Braves, were down from the Midwest hoping to witness one of baseball's most historic moments. Palmer's story had a happy ending, Reynolds' yarn a sad one.

"It was the most exciting game in baseball ever played as far as I am concerned," said Palmer over the din in Box A on the press level. "I was happy to be in on such a great occasion."

Said Reynolds, "Can you believe I came all the way from Chicago to see Aaron hit No. 715, and I was standing at the bar trying to get a drink and missed it?

"I am really embarrassed. But – can you imagine – missing Aaron's big one?"

Chub Fenney stammered and groped for words. Then he found some good ones. "Hank's 715 – it was a great moment, a fine moment for the game of baseball," said the National League president. "About Hank, I'll just have to say, class will tell. He has it."

No, Peggy Lee, that's not all there is. There was this tremendous chorus of boos when Monte Irvin, from Bowie Kuhn's office, relayed congratulations from the commissioner of all baseball. He had to be in Cleveland – to go to dinner. Sorry about that, Monte. The great Southeast bleeds for him. ⬤

Bill Bartholomay, who later sold the Braves to Ted Turner, poses with Hank Aaron and Stan Musial to celebrate Aaron's 3,000th career hit in 1970. (AP Photo)

★ ★ ★

BEYOND WORDS

The Steady Drumbeat of a Hammer

By Furman Bisher | April 9, 1974

The flower of American sporting journalism was caught with its tongue tied. With its fingers arthritic. Its brain turned into a glob of quivering gelatin. Its nervous system drawn as tight as a banjo's strings.

It had rehearsed every move, memorized every line. Then took the stage to perform and every word stuck in its throat.

Henry Louis Aaron hit the 715th home run in the 2,967th game of his major league career, and nobody had anything left to say. I mean, there just aren't 715 ways to say that Henry Aaron hit a home run. Besides, they'd worn out all the others in a long winter's anticipation, and last week when he hit No. 714 in Cincinnati.

In fact, No. 715 was only a rerun of No. 693, also hit off Al Downing in Atlanta Stadium with a man on base. And it was nothing to compare with No. 400, which cleared everything in Philadelphia and came down somewhere near Trenton. Aaron's guest of honor that night was Bo Belinsky.

There is this to be said about it: It was the first home run he has ever hit after hearing Pearl Bailey sing the national anthem. It was also an occasion added to extensively, though witlessly, by the absence of Bowie Kuhn, riotously referred to as the Commissioner of Baseball.

It was a Louisville bat against a Spalding ball, which hit a BankAmerica sign over the left-field fence and was fielded by a left-handed pitcher named Tom House. Fifty-three thousand people saw it in person, but what they weren't going to appreciate so much was when they got home they learned that with their tickets their sellout had bought free television for the other million and a half Atlantans who stayed at home. The Braves had thrown open the show for local consumption just before the field was turned into a riot of color, Americana, teary-eyed emotionalism, political swashbuckling and deafening fireworks.

Alphonse Erwin Downing has won a Babe Ruth World Series for Trenton, N.J., and pitched in a World Series for the New York Yankees. He has won 115 games, 20 in one season, and become known as a steady, reliable member of the Los Angeles Dodgers. But Monday night he carved his initials on America's memory.

He has a new cross to bear. He won't be remembered for the 115 games, but for the inside fastball that Aaron hit over the fence.

At the same time, he assured several pitchers of a

The magic number 715 appears on the wall over the head of an elated Hank Aaron during a press conference after Aaron became history's new home run king. (AP Photo)

place in posterity, a little hall of notoriety of their own. They all belong to the "We Served Henry Aaron a Home Run Club," senior member Vic Raschi, then on the shady side of a substantial career and serving it out as a St. Louis Cardinal.

The lineup of Aaron's victims is a procession of extremes, from Sandy Koufax, who was on his way to the Hall of Fame, to Joe Trimble, a Pittsburgh rookie who never won a game in the majors.

He hit No. 10 off Corky Valentine, who now may be seen around town as a cop. Then, he was a Cincinnati Red.

He hit one off an infielder, Johnny O'Brien, one of a pair of famous college basketball twins who was trying to discover a new career with the Pirates. He hit one off a Congressman, the Honorable Wilmer Mizell (R-NC). Wilmer was then "Vinegar Bend," a bumpkin rookie with a bashful smile and the kind of "Aw, shucks!" personality that made sports reporters look him up.

He hit another off Faul and off Law, and another off a Brewer, a Boozer and a Barr. One off Rabe and one off Mabe. And off Hook and Nye.

He hit 'em off Morehead and Moorhead. And R. Miller and R.L. Miller, three different Jacksons, and Veale and Lamb.

With No. 715 he assured permanent attention for handservants merely passing that way. Otherwise, Thornton Kipper, Herb Moford, John Andre, Rudy Minarcin, Tom Acker, Lino Dinoso, Art Ceccarelli and the improbable Whammy Douglas would have passed on and been forgotten. They are now forever engraved on the marble of Aaron's record like the roll of soldiers memorialized on a courthouse monument.

Naturally, one is supposed to feel that he has been witness to one of the monumental sports events of all history, if he were in the park. These things don't penetrate the perspective so soon. You're overprepared. It's not like sitting there watching this flippant youth, Cassius Clay, knock a bear like Sonny Liston out of the world heavyweight title. Or Centre College whip Harvard.

There's no shock to get your attention. No. 715 was anticipated, awaited like childbirth. It's like buying a ticket to watch a bank get robbed, or a train wreck. Everybody's so thoroughly ready that nobody can appreciate the history of it all. Even the President sat in Washington with his dialing finger exercised for action.

"He invited me to the White House," Aaron said. It is suggested that he not loiter on the way.

"Magnavox gets the ball and the bat for five years; then they go to the Hall of Fame," he said. That covered several other loose ends.

I don't want to fuel still another fire, but as I depart I feel compelled to leave with you another record in the line of fire: Aaron is well ahead of Ruth's pace the year of his 60 home runs. The Babe didn't hit his second home run until the 11th game. ⚾

The sellout crowd at Atlanta Stadium gathers to witness history on April 8, 1974. (Chuck Vollertsen/The Atlanta Journal-Constitution)

★ ★ ★
IT'S OVER

Hammerin' Hank Stands All Alone at 715

By Frank Hyland | April 9, 1974

And then there was one.

After 2,966 other games, after 11,294 other times at bat and, yes, 714 other home runs, Hank Aaron stands alone and not even the mighty, legendary Ruth can touch him.

Aaron hit home run No. 715 in the fourth inning Monday night in Atlanta Stadium off a fastball by lefthander Al Downing of the Los Angeles Dodgers and there can be no doubters. A record crowd of 53,775 saw it in person. Millions more saw it on television from Bangor, Maine, to Tokyo, Japan.

Where he hit it, over the left-center field fence some 365 feet from home plate, the sign says "Think of It as Money" and it will be money in the bank for Hank Aaron. But, it was more. Think of it as history.

For 39 years, the legend of Ruth reigned supreme. His was the one record which would withstand the test of time. But it started to crumble when a skinny Black teenager from Mobile, Alabama, stepped on a train 23 years ago with two dollars and two sandwiches in his pocket.

"Even five years ago," Aaron said, "I didn't think I'd be here."

He finally made it, though, and he made it with typical Aaron suddenness, if not in the typical Aaron style. It was his first swing of the night (he had walked his first time up) just like No. 714 was last Thursday in Cincinnati. It came on a one ball, no strike pitch. This time, though, it helped win a ball game, 7-4, for the Atlanta Braves over the Dodgers.

"I thought it had a chance," he said later, after the toasts had been toasted in the clubhouse, "but it wasn't the kind of home run I usually hit."

And, just like that, the chase of The Record was over. "Thank God it's over," Aaron told the crowd in the midst of a 10-minute ovation and ceremony.

Almost as important to Aaron was where he hit the home run. He had been hassled to play the first series in Cincinnati when he didn't want to. He was even willing to carry the weight of the pressures for another few days to make it here in Atlanta.

"It was only right to hit it here," he said. "I wanted to hit it here. I'm very happy I did."

Darrell Evans was on base when he did, there by the grace of one of five Los Angeles errors. Aaron looked at a pitch low and away. Then Downing made

Hank Aaron warms up in the infield before the start of the home opener at Atlanta Stadium against the Los Angeles Dodgers on April 8, 1974. To Aaron's great relief, he surpassed Babe Ruth's record later that night after months of anticipation. (AP Photo)

the fatal mistake, allowing a fastball he intended to have inside to get out over the plate.

And as Curt Simmons, then of Philadelphia, once said, "Trying to sneak a fastball past Henry Aaron is like trying to sneak the sun past a rooster."

He made it around the bases quicker than usual, grinning as the biggest baseball crowd in the history of the stadium roared. "At that time," he said with a grin, "I was thinking of just one thing. I wanted to touch all the bases."

Teammate Ralph Garr made sure he did, grabbing his right leg and jamming down on home plate. Then, Garr and the rest of the Braves lifted Aaron in the air while relief pitcher Tom House dashed in with the ball he had caught as it cleared the fence.

Aaron's mother was out of the special box near the Braves box and heading for her son to hug him ("I didn't know my mother could hug so tight," Aaron laughed). He went to the box where his wife and the rest of his family were seated.

Then, it was back to the field where he was congratulated by Braves chairman of the board Bill Bartholomay. More, he was congratulated for several minutes by the huge crowd.

His hat askew and a huge grin splitting his face, he waved to the crowd, acknowledging the applause. The pressure of Babe Ruth, the weight of the chase was lifted.

"Oh, man," he said, "you don't know what a weight that was off my shoulders. I'm just so happy it's over. Now, maybe I can relax. Maybe now my teammates can relax. Maybe, like Ralph Garr said, we can get back to baseball."

Aaron and the Braves might as well. The mountain has been scaled. The prize sought has been won.

The impact seemed to have set in on the crowd, the media and Aaron's teammates, but Aaron wasn't all too sure what he felt just yet.

"Maybe tomorrow when I wake up, I'll realize what has happened," he said. "Right now, it's just a home run, I'm glad we won a game and I'm glad I did something to help win it."

By the time he came out for rookie Rowland Office in the top of the eighth inning, the Dodgers had done perhaps more to help the Braves win it than Aaron. But the Dodgers had not done it with a home run and history. Hank Aaron might realize that in the morning.

He will have plenty of help remembering. The game wasn't even over yet when President Richard Nixon called with more congratulations. The clubhouse was filled with people close to the Braves and Aaron. Champagne corks were popped and the bubbly drunk. If Aaron didn't yet realize what had happened, the rest of the world did.

After over a century of baseball, he was No. 1 in the No. 1 glamour category in the game. Some future youngster won't be chasing the Babe. He'll be chasing the Hammer.

Some already know that. It showed his third time at bat, the one after the home run.

"C'mon, Supe," hollered Garr from the dugout, "Go break Hank Aaron's record!" ⚾

Hank Aaron's wife, Billye, accompanied him to the press conference following his historic game. (AP Photo)

Henry Aaron addresses fans at a Brewers-Braves exhibition game celebrating "Welcome Home Henry Night" in Milwaukee on May 7, 1974. Aaron hit 398 of his record 755 major-league home runs for the Milwaukee Braves from 1954 to 1965. (AP Photo)

TWENTY YEARS ON

A Tribute to Henry Aaron's 715th Home Run

By Thomas Stinson | April 13, 1994

Twenty years ago, Henry Aaron became baseball's home run king. On this night, the Braves pay tribute to their greatest player.

Hours before, out in left field, Bill Buckner wrestled with the wall, such as it was. It was actually a low padded cyclone fence 20 years ago and Buckner vaulted it time after time until he said he could finally get over in eight-tenths of a second. Just in case he had to go after the ball. And make no doubt, the Dodgers' left fielder would go after the ball. He planned "to jump no matter what." It would be that kind of night, Henry Aaron's night.

"Seven hundred home runs," Buckner wondered out loud. "I couldn't hit 700 home runs in batting practice, taking all day for three straight months."

At midday April 8, 1974, the Atlanta Braves said there were still 10,000 general admission tickets available for the home opener with Los Angeles. Henry Aaron had tied Babe Ruth's career home run record in Cincinnati the previous weekend, the next one making for 715, and if the rest of the world was turning out to watch, it took his hometown a spell longer to smell the coffee. By 5 p.m., Atlanta Stadium was sold out, Aaron's home run manifest destiny.

It was Phil Niekro who said Aaron's homers were "like the sun coming up. You just don't know what time."

It wouldn't be the first inning. Al Downing, a veteran Dodgers left-handed pitcher, had walked Aaron on five pitches and was dutifully booed for it. The Dodgers had flown in the night before and Downing, 32, had not gotten to bed until 3 a.m. He had never lost to Atlanta (even if Aaron had homered twice off him the season before) and with L.A. starters having given up but two runs in the season's first 27 innings, the club's pitching had been excellent. Downing was used to big games, too. A decade before, he was pitching World Series games for the New York Yankees.

"I don't think any pitcher can disregard the surroundings," Downing had said. "I'll be aware of it but I'll also be aware of what I have to do. Anyway, it's his moment, not mine."

That much was clear before any player had taken the field. A pregame salute to Aaron's career had taken 45 minutes and the normal police detail of 17 had been almost tripled to 46 to handle the crowd of 53,775, a record which stands today. The game was Aaron's 2,967th. In the fourth inning, he came to the plate for his 11,294th at-bat. It seemed inevitable. But then it didn't.

Said Aaron, "Even five years ago, I didn't think I'd be here."

Behind the plate, Joe Ferguson, the Dodgers' 27-year-old catcher, faced the night's first serious

Be it in batting practice or hitting his unforgettable 715th home run, a Hank Aaron swing was something to truly behold. (AP Photo)

problem. The Dodgers, unbeaten in three games that young season, led 3-1 but Darrell Evans, leading off the inning, had just made first on an error by shortstop Bill Russell and how Downing handled Aaron would dictate the game's direction at mid-point.

"I knew he was going to work the outside part of the plate consistently with screwballs and fastballs and things like that," Aaron said. "I had not had very good luck with him. But I was lucky enough to get into a situation where he had to pitch to me."

Still, Downing opened with a changeup that Ferguson rescued from the dirt. Ball 1.

"We could have come back with another changeup but that would have accomplished nothing," Ferguson said. "We had to even the count. We knew he was trying to pull so we wanted to go down and away from him. There's no way he's going to hit that for a homer."

So Ferguson called for a low slider. Out in the Braves bullpen, Buzz Capra had stationed himself on the fence in left-center to watch, but the crowd, now assembled for about two hours, had grown somewhat festive in the interim and scattered beer showers had compelled the Braves reliever to seek refuge. Taking his place on the fence was Tom House, a fringe reliever with the club who not only had a business administration degree from Southern Cal but a master's in marketing. Thirty feet above him in the stands, a man with a large fish net waved at Aaron. House, however, like Downing, expected Aaron to pull the ball.

On the mound, Downing took his stretch, made a token check of Evans at first and then snapped off his slider. Aaron reacted to the pitch as if cued. It was 9:07 p.m.

"It was a good pitch to throw but I didn't get it where I wanted it," Downing said. "Got it up a little too high and over too much of the plate. I just didn't get it

there. Home run hitters have a way of hitting the ball out of the park."

Aaron connected. At first glimpse, the ball did not seem particularly well hit. At shortstop, Russell even lurched as if to jump for it. Slowly, however, the ball rose toward left-center. The crowd, on its feet since Aaron had come to the plate, reached full throat. At WSB's microphone, Milo Hamilton barked " . . . that ball is gonna be . . ."

All of this fell directly into Bill Buckner's plan. As he sprinted to the wall, he worked his footing to prepare for his leap over the fence and into immortality, just as he had practiced. But the ball was carrying now, some 10 feet over his head as he hit the warning track. He leaped anyway, but at a lesser pace, reaching as he hit the fence top, his vault dying in the white noise of the outfield.

"I didn't think it had a chance of going out," he said afterward. "But it just kept going and going. You know, that's the way most of Aaron's home runs are hit. The guy's amazing. It's as if he knows exactly how far to hit them and hits them no farther."

With Buckner levitating atop the fence, House had no alternative but to catch the ball, as it was hit directly to him adjacent to the 385-foot mark. The oversized fish net swiped at it as it came down but missed, leaving House with the most expensive merchandise on the property. Sammy Davis Jr. had offered Aaron $25,000 for the ball. Three Snellville businessmen had jumped the ante to $36,000. The Motorola manufacturing company had a $1 million deal with Aaron that would involve the ball and bat making a victory tour around America. And suddenly, Tom House held the treasure in his own fist.

"This is my one moment of glory," he said in the clubhouse. "I can't believe all the attention I'm getting."

While the ball from home run number 715 was a highly prized piece of baseball memorabilia, Hank Aaron's signature was also among the most sought-after autographs for sports fans and collectors alike. (AP Photo).

Aaron, against his custom, watched the ball clear the wall as he ran and was first congratulated by the Dodgers' Steve Garvey at first, Davey Lopes at second and a couple fans who had trespassed as he turned for third. Ron Cey, then just a second-year third baseman, let him pass in deference, saying, "He's Hank Aaron. I'm just another ball player."

The scene at home started as a celebration, became a team meeting and then degenerated into a roving media fest as Aaron found his mother Estella on the way to the dugout and squeezed her. The game stopped for 11 minutes and Downing went to plate umpire Satch Davidson to ask permission to go sit in the dugout. Monte Irvin, representing the conspicuously absent commissioner Bowie Kuhn, presented Aaron with a $3,000 diamond and gold watch. For a while, it drizzled. Some 100 telegrams arrived at the stadium before the game was concluded. President Nixon called.

Somewhere in the middle of the crowd, House found Aaron, having sprinted in from the bullpen. The Braves had imprinted the game balls with infrared labels, ensuring that No. 715 could be positively identified. In the crowd, the kid pitcher pressed that one-and-only ball into Aaron's hand.

Grabbing a microphone, the game's new home run king said, "It was only right to hit it here. I wanted to hit it here. I'm very happy I did."

If the moment stands still, the night itself raced on faster than life. Once play resumed, Downing walked two men and was pulled, cabbing back to the hotel before the game was over. The stadium was less than half full when Aaron (2-for-3, 2 RBI, 1 run) was substituted for in the eighth by Rowland Office. Atlanta won 7-4. The work crews were still stashing the bunting outside when one addled newsman asked Aaron what was next, overtaking Stan Musial for second place on the all-time hits list?

"Yeah," said Aaron late that night, "I really have to concentrate on my batting average." ◗

New York City Mayor Abe Beame receives an autographed baseball and the commemorative bat presented to the city by Hank Aaron outside City Hall in June 1974. The home run king was presented with the city's Gold Medal and made an honorary citizen. (AP Photo)

ECHOES OF NO. 715

Time for a Reminder of Aaron's Eminence

By Steve Hummer | April 14, 1994

Twenty years and five nights ago – back when it was actually possible to park near the stadium – Hank Aaron hit an epic home run. A 40-year-old man made his 715th circumnavigation of the bases, then was greeted at the end by a small riot and an invitation to lay down a great burden.

The echoes of that night could be picked up again Wednesday, in the film clips and the speeches and the knickknacks of an anniversary tribute to a career long on years, talent and air miles.

They are fainter, to be sure. Aaron brought his father to Wednesday's affair – and also his grandchildren.

No, it doesn't seem like just yesterday that he broke the mythic Babe's home run record. Not even the night before. On the evening of No. 715, Ryan Klesko was a 2-year-old in swaddling. David Justice was getting ready to turn 8, watching the spectacle on a small black-and-white television in his room.

Put one ear to the ground, though, and there are vibrations from that distant night. Every 20 years or so, you need to be reminded of Hank Aaron's life in baseball.

"I'm glad I'm here to see it," said San Francisco Giants manager Dusty Baker, in town for a little business this week. Baker was on deck for the Braves 20 years and five nights ago. "I'm surprised it took this long. I think it takes time for something so great to soak in."

Baker speaks like a manager now when considering the player Aaron. The career total of 755 home runs becomes but one line of a complete scouting report.

"Look at the hits [3,771]; he was a great hitter," Baker said. "And the [2,297] RBIs. That's what was amazing. And you lose sight of what an outstanding outfielder he was. And what a great baserunner he was. He very rarely made a mistake."

"More than the home runs," Aaron said, "I was proud of the other things I could do on a ballfield."

That said, a third-filled stadium – couldn't they have waited for the house to fill – would not have so loudly saluted Aaron for his baserunning. The home runs are what float his boat. They are the measure of 23 years spent terrorizing pitchers in Milwaukee and Atlanta.

Asked who was his toughest out, Sandy Koufax never hesitated.

"Bad Henry," he said.

So many home runs that when laid on top of one another, they make this statistical wall that appears too tall to scale. Today's players just bounce off and go looking for tax shelters.

It's difficult to foresee the modern player who would challenge Aaron's record. Who would linger so

Hank Aaron stands with Cincinnati Reds manager and former Braves teammate Dusty Baker and his son Darren Baker, as the national anthem plays during the Civil Rights Game ceremony before a game between the Chicago White Sox and the Cincinnati Reds at Great American Ball Park, in Cincinnati in 2009. (AP Photo)

long, after earning two or three fortunes in their prime? Aaron hit 42 of his home runs after his 40th birthday. By then, the '90s' player should own his own country.

The investment in such a record is staggering. Over the past five years, nobody has more home runs than Fred McGriff. He hit one more Wednesday, hauntingly close to the sign marking Aaron's record-breaker, to beat the Giants in 12 innings and push his career total to 230. Just another 15 years at a pace of 35 a year, and the 30-year-old McGriff will match Aaron.

"Hank's been taking care of me since I've been here," said McGriff, who dresses next to Aaron's old locker, sealed and containing only a baseball, a raincoat and a tray of rat poison.

We'll go out on a narrow ledge and say McGriff doesn't quite break Aaron's record. Simply because he doesn't have to play that long to survive.

"I was still hungry," Aaron said, "and you do some crazy things when you're still hungry."

There just is no reason for the new age star to maintain that same edge.

For example, Justice dreams of retiring to some faraway island when he's 35. The great Barry Bonds holds no aspirations of a career long enough to assault 755.

"I just want to make the Hall of Fame, however long it takes," he said. "When they say you're in, I'm gone."

The record sleeps safely, because the effort is now judged even more unrealistic. The monument of 715 – then 755 – has only grown by today's standards. Said Justice, "That's why he's Hank Aaron, All World."

One does need to hear that every 20 years or so. ◗

Sandy Koufax called Hank Aaron "Bad Henry" and said he was his toughest out, high praise from the legendary lefty pitcher. (AP Photo)

DEMOCRACY DELIVERS

City Council to Honor Aaron with Stretch of Capitol Avenue

By Dave Kindred | February 26, 1997

A man with a prophet's beard, a man wearing a Yankee cap, a man with an orange lapel button announcing his political candidacy and the promise, "I Won't Make a Deal" – this man named Dave Walker marched double-time to the lectern and on his way said to Jared Samples, the Atlanta city councilman chairing the meeting, "I know you don't like me, Mr. Chairman."

Good day to you, too, Mr. Walker.

For 15 years, Walker says, he has worked as a street vendor at Five Points. Only recently he decided to run for the presidency of the Atlanta City Council. As most quixotic campaigns are equal parts eloquence and bombast, so is Walker's.

And there he was at City Hall on that Tuesday morning to say his piece about Hank Aaron, which we'll get to in a minute.

As well it should, the council continues its attempt to honor Aaron, the greatest home run hitter in baseball history. The new ballpark should have been named for Aaron. No surprise, though, when the Braves named it Turner Field, honoring the man who signs the paychecks, Ted Turner.

Now the council has proposed changing the name of part of Capitol Avenue. From Fulton Street to Ormond, those long blocks alongside the ballpark complex, the avenue would become Hank Aaron Drive.

Shortly before 10 o'clock Tuesday morning, Sonia Gilbert, a citizen of Atlanta, sat alone in a committee meeting room, waiting to tell the politicians what she thought.

She thought this: "I resent the Braves not naming the whole stadium after Aaron. It was Hank Aaron who did all the work, who hit the home runs. Ted Turner needs more glory? He is world-wide known and is married to a world-wide actress. He needs more?

"And Hank Aaron, now they want to give him part of Capitol Avenue? Why not all of it?"

Thirty-six years ago, Sonia Gilbert said, her grandfather opened the Kozy Home Company hardware store next to the family home at 674 Capitol Ave. There was a post office in the store. She lived on Capitol in 1964 when the city put up the old ballpark it now intends to tear down.

"Everybody thought, with the old ballpark, that the whole area would be developed into something, but nothing was done then, and nothing will be done now," Gilbert said. "Our family would still be living there, but we couldn't make a living. Finally, we tore down the house because it had been vandalized too much."

That meeting by the public utilities committee was expected to end with the formality of a vote sending the Aaron proposal to the full City Council.

Then Sonia Gilbert went to the lectern and told

Hank Aaron during a post-game ceremony after the final game was played in Atlanta-Fulton County Stadium on September 23, 1996. (David Tulis/The Atlanta Journal-Constitution)

the council members that she, as a property owner on Capitol Avenue, had no objection to the name change, except this: "All of Capitol Avenue should be named for him. He's the one who did all the hitting and running."

Well. Democracy works. And soon enough, Councilman Rob Pitts said of Gilbert's speech, "It's a good point."

Then came Douglas Dean, a community activist in the ballpark neighborhood. He, too, liked the idea of renaming a greater length of Capitol Avenue. Extending Hank Aaron Drive to Jonesboro Road "would add value" to real estate along the street, said Dean.

At which point came the bearded entrepreneur Dave Walker in his Yankee cap. ("Nothing against the Braves. When I was a kid, I always watched the Yankees beat the Dodgers in the World Series.") With a glance at Chairman Samples, who once ordered the raucous gadfly removed from a council meeting, Walker moved to the lectern where he adopted a casual pose, leaning on an elbow, and said this Hank Aaron stuff was all too much.

"No Black elected official running for office is going to oppose this," he said. "But I'm running and I oppose it… Mr. Aaron has a statue. Mr. Aaron has the record. Mr. Aaron is collecting a salary. Mr. Aaron has, in my opinion, gotten as much out of his 755 home runs as he can expect to get."

Well. Democracy works. No one paid any attention at all to Walker.

Instead, the meeting ended with a call for another public hearing. That one, on March 11, will consider whether to put Hank Aaron's name on Capitol Avenue all the way from Fulton Street to Jonesboro Road, maybe two miles in all, a long drive even by Hammerin' Hank's standards. ◗

Top: The funeral procession for Hank Aaron makes its way along Hank Aaron Drive and turns toward the site of the former Atlanta-Fulton County Stadium. After a nearly three-hour funeral service on Jan. 27, 2021, the hearse carrying Aaron detoured off the road bearing his name to swing through the former site. (AP Photo) Opposite: Henry Frantz plays the bagpipes at Truist Park during "A Celebration of Henry Louis Aaron," a memorial service celebrating the life and enduring legacy of the late Hall of Famer and American icon on Jan. 26, 2021. (AP Photo)

HANK AARON DRIVE

Turner Field Finally Gets a New Address
By Michelle Hiskey | April 1997

For months, the letterhead on the Atlanta Braves' new stationery has boasted the team's illustrious new address at Turner Field.

This morning, the city makes it official by dedicating Hank Aaron Drive and unveiling a new street sign at the northeast corner of the ballpark.

Turner Field's address is 755 Hank Aaron Drive, referring to the slugger's career home run total. Hank Aaron Drive replaces a stretch of Capitol Avenue from Ralph David Abernathy Boulevard to McDonough Boulevard.

"We can't think of any better way to honor our hometown baseball hero than naming this portion of the street for him, one day before the home opener," said Nick Gold, spokesman for Mayor Bill Campbell, who will speak at the event. Aaron and his family will attend, along with Braves executives. ◗

LONG TIME COMING

Aaron Finally Gets Recognition for Feat, Career

By Mark Bradley | April 9, 1999

"Thank God it's over," he'd said that night, but it never really was. At 9:07 p.m. on April 8, 1974, Henry Louis Aaron had hit his 715th home run. It should have been a moment of transcendence. That it somehow was not has taken a quarter-century to sort out.

"This makes up for all that didn't happen then," said Billye Aaron, a relative newlywed on the night her husband supplanted George Herman Ruth. Twenty-five years later, she sat before a media throng at a new stadium across the street, watching as Major League Baseball unveiled the Hank Aaron Award. Speaking of the Aarons, commissioner Bud Selig said: "I wish they'd had a happier experience."

Seven hundred fifteen home runs bought Hank Aaron space in the record book of our national pastime, but it didn't bring him satisfaction. Race is invariably identified as the culprit, though it's worth recalling that when Babe Ruth's other hallowed mark was broken it brought that new holder no peace, either. And Roger Maris was white.

Hank Aaron was not. Hank Aaron received racist mail that he keeps still. The endorsements that figured to gush toward baseball's all-time home run champion were a comparative trickle. Bowie Kuhn, then the game's commissioner, wasn't there that fateful night 25 years ago, keeping instead a commitment to address the Wahoo Club in Cleveland.

"I broke one of the most prestigious records," Aaron said Thursday, "but was baseball ready to accept it? I don't think America was ready to accept it."

Said Frank Robinson, an Aaron contemporary on hand this night: "I don't know if America's ready for it now."

America might or might not be. Baseball assuredly is. Twenty-five years after the fact, baseball wants Hank Aaron to share in the honeyed glow that washed over Mark McGwire and Sammy Sosa last summer. Baseball wants to say it's sorry for any and all slights. "I don't believe (No. 715) got either the attention or the depth of feeling it deserved," Selig said. Baseball wants to rectify that.

So now, ex post facto, baseball is trying to make Aaron's feat a moment of McGwire/Sosa warm fuzziness. It is honoring No. 715 in a way it didn't salute, say, the silver anniversary of Maris' 61st. The president of these United States flew in for his 65th birthday in February. "I didn't have to go to his house," said Aaron, still disbelieving. "He came to me."

On the 25th anniversary of hitting his 715th home run, Hank Aaron shows off the newly unveiled Hank Aaron Award, given annually to the best overall offensive performer in each league. (AP Photo)

On Thursday, the lords of baseball came to Atlanta 25 years after Bowie Kuhn went to Cleveland. (Though Ted Turner, who owns the Braves, was conspicuously elsewhere. He was thought to be overseas. Is there a Wahoo Club in Helsinki?) Pre-ceremony, Aaron posed with the award minted in his name, gladly obliging the dozen photographers who kept calling, "Look over here." The on-field celebration was heartfelt all around. Said Aaron: "This night tops it all."

And then he and his wife took a victory lap in a golf cart, a sweet moment long deferred but ultimately not denied. "Thank God it's over," he'd said that night, but 25 years later Henry Louis Aaron seemed gratified that the transcendental part was, at blessed last, just beginning. ◐

Above: Hank Aaron with fellow 1982 Baseball Hall of Fame inductee Frank Robinson. (AP Photo) Opposite: Hank Aaron is flanked by past Hank Aaron Award winners Alex Rodriguez (right) and David Ortiz (left) prior to Game 2 of the 2019 World Series between the Houston Astros and the Washington Nationals. (AP Photo)

HITTING HIS STRIDE

Years After Breaking Home Run Record, Aaron Makes Name for Himself in Business World

By Jim Auchmutey | February 1, 2004

They say you couldn't sneak a fastball past Hank Aaron. Apparently you can't sneak much else past him either.

Not long after Aaron opened his first Church's Chicken franchise in Atlanta's West End, he took a seat in the dining room to study the operation, much as he used to study pitchers from the on-deck circle. He noticed an employee toting crates of uncooked poultry to a truck. He took another look and it hit him: That man's stealing my chicken!

"What," Aaron thought, "have I gotten myself into now?"

He can afford to chuckle as he tells the story now, a decade later, over coffee at a new Krispy Kreme doughnut shop around the corner from that Church's. They're both part of his 755 Restaurant Corp., which owns 19 fast-food outlets in Georgia and the Carolinas, with more on the way. He's also the majority partner in six auto dealerships, which he oversees from his office at Hank Aaron BMW and Mini in Union City.

As he prepared to celebrate his 70th birthday in 2004, the most famous athlete in Atlanta history says that he feels less like an old ballplayer than a businessman hitting his stride.

"To be honest with you, I was scared when I retired from baseball," Aaron says. "I wasn't sure I was ever going to make good money again."

So what kind of money is he worth now?

"A little," Aaron says. "I couldn't say how much."

His sly smile indicates it's good to be the home run king.

Aaron concedes that he made some expensive mistakes along the road to prosperity – including a near bankruptcy years ago – but he learned from every stumble, just as he used to learn from his strikeouts. In some ways, friends say, his business successes have been as satisfying for him as his playing career.

"I think Hank has enjoyed the last 20 years of his life as much as he enjoyed baseball," says the man who got him into restaurants, Frank Belatti, chairman of AFC Enterprises, the parent company of Church's and Popeyes chicken. "Hank wanted to be known for something besides hitting a baseball. He wanted to be respected as an entrepreneur."

Nearly 150 of Aaron's friends and associates gathered to celebrate his latest milestone at a private dinner. The guest of honor had changed a little in the 30 years since he broke Babe Ruth's career home run record.

The feared hitter Sandy Koufax once called "Bad Henry" goes by a different nickname these days; to his five grandchildren, he's Pa-Pa. He wears glasses now and takes medication for his blood pressure. Though he

As Hank Aaron approached his 70th birthday in February 2004, his 755 Restaurant Corp. owned 19 fast-food outlets, and he was also the majority partner in six auto dealerships. (Joey Ivansco/The Atlanta Journal-Constitution)

works to stay in shape, he's thicker around the middle, carrying about 30 pounds more than his playing weight of 185. When Billye Aaron, his wife of three decades, suggested he join her on the South Beach Diet, he resisted. He does try to avoid fried foods, having decided Satchel Paige was right: They "anger up" the blood.

"He's mellowed a great deal," Billye Aaron says of her husband. "It's amazing how his interests have changed. I think he would have enjoyed business earlier, but the opportunities didn't come."

Aaron occasionally talks about retiring and wants to spend more time at the couple's second home on a golf course in West Palm Beach, Florida. He does fewer speaking engagements and baseball memorabilia shows because he doesn't enjoy traveling as much as he used to. Yet he still keeps a schedule that would tire a man half his age.

When Aaron's in town, his routine begins well before 6 a.m. as he leaves the large brick home he built 30 years ago on a lake in the Southwest neighborhood of Atlanta. He heads to Turner Field for a pre-dawn workout in the players' weight room. As a senior vice president with the Braves, he keeps an office there, but baseball claims less of his attention nowadays.

"I could see them needing me more at spring training this year because of the cutback in payroll," Aaron says. "They're going to have more kids down there, and some of them are thirsty for advice. But some of the players these days, they walk in with a suitcase full of money and a cellphone against their head – I can't tell them anything."

Aaron, the best-paid player in baseball near the end of his career, never made more than $240,000 a year. Texas Rangers slugger Alex Rodriguez makes more than that in two games.

After his workout – at least 30 minutes on the treadmill, followed by weightlifting – Aaron showers and dresses in a double-breasted checked suit. He hops into his navy blue BMW 745 sedan, walkie-talkie in hand, and drives past a couple of his properties. First stop: the Krispy Kreme he opened a year and a half ago in the West End to replace a time-worn shop down the street.

"I am very proud of this place," Aaron says, taking a booth near the "Hot Doughnuts Now" sign in the window. "I'm proud because we built it on this side of town. There was talk about moving it. People want nice things here just like they want in Buckhead or anywhere else."

Margaret Wolfe, who has worked at the shop and its predecessor for 27 years, is grateful it stayed in the neighborhood. "I get Mr. Aaron his coffee every morning," she says. He knows that she just turned 73 and has arthritis.

Aaron orders a doughnut – they bring him two – and settles in to talk about what he's learned about business. It isn't complicated: hire good people, sweat the details, be patient, deal only with those who earn your trust. As he speaks, he's constantly interrupted by well-wishers who want to shake his hand or ask for an autograph. Whenever such intrusions irritate him, he recalls a woman at the airport pointing him out to her daughter.

"That's Hank Aaron," she said.

"I thought he was dead," the little girl replied.

"I'd rather have people see me sitting here like an ordinary Joe than have them wonder if I'm still alive," Aaron said with a laugh.

Owning a business was the furthest thing from Aaron's mind when he was growing up in Mobile. One of eight children, the son of a dockworker, all he cared about was playing baseball – especially after he heard about Jackie Robinson.

Aaron left Mobile in 1952, at 18, and signed for $200 a month with the Indianapolis Clowns of the Negro Leagues. Fourteen years later he returned to the South as a superstar when the Braves moved from Milwaukee to Atlanta. He soon had a contract for $100,000. For the first time, he had enough money to think about investing.

His initial efforts were clumsy, to say the least. "I was easy, just like so many athletes today," Aaron says. "It's tough when you don't know anything about nothin' and you have all this money."

One of his first ventures was a barbecue joint in southwest Atlanta. Hammerin' Hank's was supposed to be the flagship for a chain of restaurants, but the white businessmen in charge of the enterprise had a

Hank Aaron was determined to succeed beyond the baseball field, overcoming early entrepreneurial mistakes to achieve great success in the business world. (Marlene Karas/The Atlanta Journal-Constitution)

fundamentally flawed concept.

"They wanted to sell chopped barbecue," Aaron says. "I told them there wasn't any such thing in this neighborhood; you had to put meat on the bone – ribs. They didn't listen to me, and they went out of business."

Another time, a man he met in Florida talked him into speculating on sugar futures. "I put up $5,000 and doubled my money, but he was just setting me up for the kill," Aaron says. "Next time he wanted more." Total loss: $20,000.

The most expensive misadventure was a real estate enterprise in the early '70s. Aaron had become baseball's first $200,000 player and was getting peppered with business propositions. He turned his affairs over to a couple of financial managers he'd rather not call by name. He gave them power of attorney and had his paychecks sent directly to them. They invested his money in real estate, most of it in an office complex near Perimeter Mall, just as Atlanta was sinking into its worst recession in decades.

Aaron's secretary had doubts about the deal and persuaded him to call in an auditor. When the auditor went to see the duo, their office had been vacated.

"I was wiped out," Aaron says. "It was a bad time to invest in real estate, and here I was doing it and losing my butt."

He put his losses at close to $1 million – his life's savings. Aaron considered legal action and went to see a lawyer, but they could find no grounds for action. The lawyer raised the possibility of filing for bankruptcy, but Aaron said no.

"I was angry, but I wasn't helpless," he says. "I still had my name and had time to recoup. I just decided to be more careful with my money."

Aaron had just broken the home run record, and his earning power was at its peak. A five-year, $1 million endorsement contract from Magnavox helped salve his wounds.

After Aaron retired as a player in 1976, Braves owner Ted Turner hired him as director of the team's minor league system. Aaron didn't risk another major business undertaking until he became an Arby's franchisee in Milwaukee in the mid-'80s. He has since sold those restaurants. ◗

A PORTRAIT OF LONGEVITY

Henry Aaron Turns 80 in Fitting Style

By Steve Hummer | February 1, 2014

Henry Aaron turns 80 on Wednesday, a long life now divided neatly in half by the 40 years building to home run No. 715 and the 40 years spent in service to that epic swing.

Time to celebrate the fully experienced life, one that has enjoyed equal meaning on both sides of the foul pole.

Aaron's 80th will not pass quietly. In Washington this week, baseball's all-natural home run king will be honored at a Friday night dinner thrown by his buddy, Commissioner Bud Selig. On Saturday, he and his likeness will be celebrated at the Smithsonian's National Portrait Gallery.

Space in that hall is reserved not only for those who can hit the fastball, but those who have, on a grander scale, influenced a nation's culture. The Hammer did his share of societal shaping with a 33-ounce piece of sculpted ash.

"Can we tell the story of baseball without Henry Aaron? I don't think so," Bethany Bentley, a gallery spokeswoman, said. He'll keep eclectic company, hanging next to actor Morgan Freeman.

The artist who did this and another portrait of Aaron to go in the Baseball Hall of Fame, Atlanta's Ross Rossin, felt it his responsibility to capture "the positive energy that comes from him, the magnetism, the charisma.

"He is more than a sports star; he is an unbelievable human being who represents the time he lived in," Rossin said. Aaron will be Rossin's fourth subject displayed at the Smithsonian, along with Freeman, former U.N. ambassador/Atlanta mayor Andrew Young and poet Maya Angelou.

Even someone who has been honored in nearly every conceivable fashion still can be moved by an event of this scale.

"I was there with Andrew Young when they hung his (portrait)," Aaron said last week. "You're on a different level when you get there. You've achieved a lot and somebody upstairs loves you. I don't know – you feel like somebody special."

Before leaving for D.C., Aaron sat for an interview in the southwest Atlanta home he has lived in since 1974. What emerged was another portrait of an octogenarian sporting icon at ease with the sum of his life.

Aaron doesn't use the tennis court at his home anymore, and in fact jokes about turning it into a garden. Doesn't fish the five-acre pond out back of the house. But otherwise, "I feel good, I really do," he said.

Travel can wear him out, but he knows he would

Hall of Famer Reggie Jackson offers his best wishes to Hank Aaron at a reception celebrating his 80th birthday. (AP Photo)

feel it all the more had he fully indulged in the pleasures of the road while he was playing.

"I feel fortunate. I feel proud of myself. I've tried to stay healthy all my life, tried to do the right things," Aaron said.

His parents willed him a long life. His father, Herbert, lived to the age of 89. Estella, his mother, made it to 96.

"I wish I knew (the secret to longevity)," he said. "Even when I played baseball, I always felt like I had to take care of myself. If I felt like the night before I stayed out a little later and it kept me from playing the kind of baseball I wanted to play, then nobody had to tell me the next night – or the next two weeks – that I had to get to bed."

There was nobody doing portraits of Aaron when he grew up in Mobile, Alabama, the third of a shipyard worker's eight children.

Birthday parties were for other kids. Aaron cannot recall any single birthday present from his childhood that left an impression.

There is a sort of pride when he speaks about the humbleness of his background, a wry humor when he declares, "I tell a lot of people I was a vegetarian before they knew what a vegetarian was. We didn't eat meat but once every two or three weeks."

He never played high school baseball. Certainly never came up playing any kind of organized youth baseball. When he left home to prove himself in the now-long-defunct Negro Leagues, he held the bat wrong (cross-handed) and contradicted his athletic ability by running on his heels rather than his toes. Such a baseball upbringing is unlikely to be duplicated in the ever-refined future.

A portion of the wall over which Aaron launched the ball that broke Babe Ruth's revered record stands a lonely watch in a parking lot across the street from Turner Field. That's pretty much all that's left of Atlanta-Fulton County Stadium, a faint echo of Aaron's past.

A prerogative of age is an almost instinctual resistance to change. He said he shed a tear when the old stadium was imploded. He'll be saddened as well when the Braves bug out of Turner Field for their new suburban Elysium.

"I never played baseball in that park, but it seems I'm connected to it somehow," Aaron said.

"You have people come along, a younger generation, who have no (sense of) history, no care about what happened there. That stadium should always be (at its current site), I think."

As for the preserved section of Atlanta-Fulton County Stadium, the relic from the historic night of April 8, 1974, when Aaron passed Ruth? "I don't know what's going to happen to that little wall. Might end up in somebody's living room," he said.

"To be honest with you, (Eddie) Mathews, (Warren) Spahn and I are getting a little lonesome up there by ourselves," Aaron said of the previous generation of Braves in the Hall of Fame.

A wave of purely Atlanta-minted Braves will be inducted into the Hall of Fame this summer when Bobby Cox, Tom Glavine and Greg Maddux (and to some extent Joe Torre) are granted prime Cooperstown real estate.

As one of the more esteemed members of the Hall, Aaron gives this latest group his hardiest endorsement.

Ah, but the unavoidable question to one of the greatest hitters ever: What could he have done against a Maddux or a Glavine in his prime?

Being 80 doesn't mean you concede a thing.

"Hitting against those guys certainly would have presented a problem, but I think that we would have had an understanding," Aaron said with a sly smile. "In my time I hit against people like (Sandy) Koufax and (Don) Drysdale and (Bob) Gibson and (Juan)

Hank Aaron reflects on his life and career prior to his 80th birthday in 2014. (Curtis Compton/The Atlanta Journal-Constitution)

Marichal, and I held my own."

Aaron hit more home runs off Drysdale (17) than any other pitcher. He hit .362 vs. Koufax, with a .647 slugging percentage. Had eight home runs and hit .288 lifetime against Marichal. He nicked Gibson for eight homers despite hitting just .215 off him. Hall of Famers all.

The contrast to this year's overflowing Hall of Fame program was the 2013 ceremony that included not a single player. That sadly hollow agenda was the product of the steroids era, so many of its stars tainted.

Perhaps the less said about the whole sorry chapter the better.

One thing Aaron definitely is not qualified to speak on is short-cuts.

We'll let it go at this: "I kind of feel sorry for what happened. … When you look at the whole situation and think about steroids, the game was made to be played right. And if you can't play it right, you shouldn't play it at all."

Letters that deserved no more than the flame of the fireplace or the muck of the landfill are boxed in Aaron's attic. He kept some of the good ones, too, the ones that urged him up and over Ruth's record.

The vile and racist scrawl sent him in the 1970s, the death threats, that is the indelible stain on Aaron's story. He would hit 40 more home runs in his professional denouement, but it was No. 715 that extruded the best and worst from the era.

Not that Aaron even glances at any of the old correspondence anymore. He just can't throw it out.

Forty years removed from the moment, Aaron still wishes he could have savored it more.

"The hardest thing I went through was the fact I was so isolated. I didn't go out to dinner. My kids had to go to a private school. I had to slip out of the back door of ballparks.

"My teammates would stay in one hotel, and I would stay in another one. Paul Casanova was a catcher with the Braves at the time. After we'd play a night game he would have to bring my dinner to my hotel if I wanted to eat anything."

Where others in search of one benchmark or another may have enjoyed the chase, Aaron looks back on the build-up to 715 and says, "I had no great moments."

Note to the generations of fans who never witnessed Aaron in a uniform: He did more than hit a baseball into the seats. He ranks third all-time in number of hits. First in RBIs, extra-base hits and total bases. Fourth in runs. Had three Gold Gloves.

The numbers, though, start to lose their sharp edge over the decades. Stats are incomplete measures of a life, cold figures telling a two-dimensional tale. They don't, for instance, account for his children's charity – the Chasing the Dream Foundation – in which Aaron takes such pride.

They don't make him smile like his five grandchildren and his one great-grandchild. "I have a granddaughter now who's at Michigan, and I told my wife, 'Wouldn't it be nice for me if I can hang around here for four more years to see her graduate?'" he said.

Aaron chased down a record compiled when those of his skin tone could not step foot on a major league field. And in the process shined a light on the dark alcoves of ignorance. What number can express that?

"I think overall my life has been good, and God has been good to me. I've tried to live my life, in spite of some things that may have happened a few years ago, by doing unto others as I'd have them do unto me," Aaron said.

"We've tried to help some of those who need help. I've been fortunate to do a lot of things in my lifetime. And I don't think I've made that many enemies."

This is the chosen week to stand back and admire the portrait of an American original. Best of all, the subject remains a fully animated work of art. ◑

Hank Aaron holds a ball autographed by the baseball legend. (Curtis Compton/The Atlanta Journal-Constitution)

A HUMBLE HERO

Hank Aaron Honored on His 80th Birthday

By Kevin Riley | February 16, 2014

It's nearly impossible to capture the stature of Hank Aaron as American icon, Atlanta community pillar and the man who broke the most revered record in sports. It's certainly hard for me, a lifelong baseball fan and an unabashed admirer of Aaron. But let's try.

Last weekend Aaron was honored on the occasion of his 80th birthday. Major League Baseball and its commissioner held a reception at the historic Hay-Adams Hotel across from the White House. The Smithsonian unveiled his portrait, and at the public event hundreds had to be turned away for lack of space to accommodate them. A celebrity-sprinkled crowd of about 350 attended a black-tie dinner at the National Portrait Gallery.

But nothing demonstrated Aaron's stature more than this:

At the black-tie event, seated near the back and just one table from me was Franco Harris. If you're not a sports fan, here's what you need to know about Harris: he was a star running back for the Pittsburgh Steeler teams of the late 1970s that won the Super Bowl four times. He's in the Pro Football Hall of Fame.

In almost any room, Harris is THE celebrity.

But on this night, as the event ended and the crowd slowly exited, Harris worked his way to the front of the room. Finally he arrived near the dais.

He wanted to get a picture with Hank Aaron.

I noticed because I was doing the same thing, as were many others at the event.

Much has been chronicled about Aaron's historic pursuit of Babe Ruth's career home run record, which Aaron broke on April 8, 1974.

There were many angles to the story of Aaron's pursuit, and it was a journey that captured the nation's attention.

He was chasing the great Ruth. The New York Yankee. The embodiment of American sport and celebrity. The symbol of baseball's golden age.

It was North against South. An ambitious, upstart city taking something away from the country's biggest city. It was Atlanta, the city that had stolen the Braves from Milwaukee, establishing itself as a true Major League town.

And it was a Black man looking to better the record of a white man, at a time when tensions around race stubbornly refused to fall away. And that part, as has been well-documented, was ugly.

At the center of this uniquely American historical drama stood the calm and stoic main character: a humble ballplayer from Mobile, Alabama.

Anyone who knew baseball could see Aaron would break the record. That was clear for some time, and especially when the previous season ended. And there is no argument about whether he was a better all-around player than Ruth.

Hank Aaron speaks at the reception honoring his 80th birthday in February 2014, in Washington, D.C. (AP Photo)

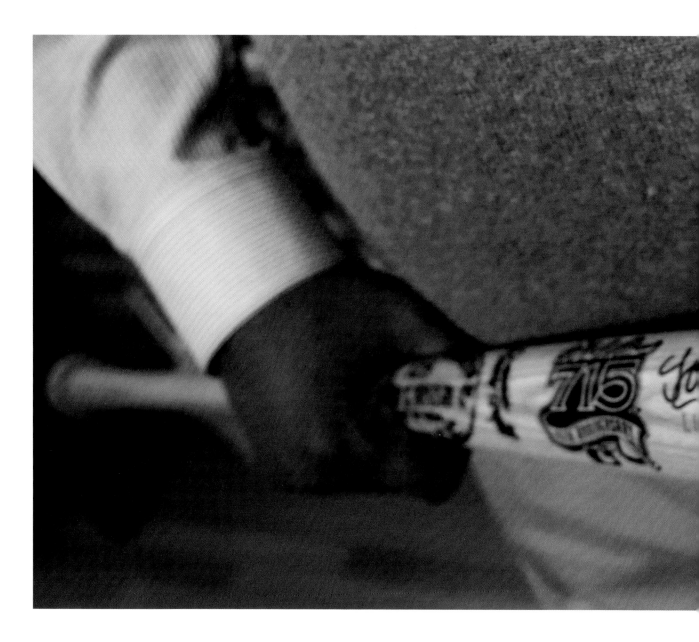

But when he broke the record, the world didn't yet know how well-suited he was for his role. How gracefully he would grab hold of history. And how he would carry its responsibility for four decades with a pristine rectitude.

It became clear during the events around Aaron's 80th birthday just how deeply respected he is, in baseball, in business and in the Atlanta community. He has never let us down, an exceedingly rare thing among celebrities, especially those in sports. Just ask someone from Cincinnati about the pain Pete Rose's descent caused that community.

Aaron's stature has only grown over the years, as the depth of his character has become clearer. His home run record is even more respected now because of Major League Baseball's struggle to ban performance enhancing drugs.

At each event last weekend, as speaker after speaker lauded him, Aaron thanked them.

A pantheon of African-American baseball stars got up and talked about how Aaron had inspired them.

When his turn to speak came, he didn't talk about baseball or his records. He didn't recount the ugly racism expressed in letters he received as he pursued

Hank Aaron holds a 715 limited edition Henry Aaron Louisville Slugger bat commemorating his record-breaking home run. (Curtis Compton/The Atlanta Journal-Constitution)

the record. He never emphasized the exhausting scrutiny he endured.

He spoke of his parents. He said he wished they could be there. "They always taught me and all of my siblings that the thing I want you to remember is, 'Do unto others as you would have them do unto you,'" he said. "That's been my philosophy."

He remarked on all the good fortune he'd enjoyed, and how so many fine people had been part of his life.

He said he was glad they could be there.

And he took a picture with Franco Harris, and anyone else who asked. Including me. And for all of us, it was the thrill of a lifetime to meet the guy who will always be a hero.

Hank Aaron in the 755 Club at Turner Field for the unveiling of the Wheaties box bearing his image in January 2002. (Jeremy Bales/The Atlanta Journal-Constitution)

A MAN OF THE PEOPLE

Fans Share Their Personal Stories of the Baseball Hero and Everyman

By Ernie Suggs | January 25, 2021

Atlanta lost a legend when Hank Aaron died in his Atlanta home at the age of 86. Though one of the greatest baseball players ever, a Hall of Famer, he also was much more. A neighbor. A friend. A supporter. A regular guy, who never refused a photograph, autograph or handshake. The Atlanta Journal-Constitution asked fans of Aaron to send in stories of their encounters with him.

BRITTANY MACKEY: A GASP

I was headed to Cooperstown for (Atlanta Braves pitcher John Smoltz's) induction. I walked on the plane and gasped when I saw Hank Aaron already seated on the plane. I asked to take a pic with him. He was kind, friendly and ever the gentleman.

I thanked him for his life and legacy, both on and off the field, and moved on. I saw him again on the way back to Atlanta. He asked me how I enjoyed Cooperstown. He told me to have a nice flight back and off we went. I'll never forget it.

LEN ROBERTS: SUPPORT THROUGH TRAGEDY

My friendship with Hank spans over 35 years. We have been in business together, been together with our families, at birthdays and weddings and on vacations. And yes, we have supported each other through tragedies. I will never forget the time when Hank gave Laurie and me the strength while our daughter, Dawn, was fighting for her life.

As a pedestrian, Dawn was hit by a drunk driver and sustained horrific injuries. Hank made sure that the ICU hospital staff were giving her the best of care.

Yeah, a few signed baseballs helped the cause. Not a few ... MANY!

PRINCESS WILKES: A STEAK MAN

I met Hank Aaron in late 2010 while working for a media research firm as a field interviewer. Unbeknownst to me, the work led me directly to his home. Shocked when I saw him, he was very gracious and said come back tomorrow when he had more time. The next day, we had so much fun conducting the interview that he invited me to come back.

Over the next week or so, he showed me some of the souvenirs he had collected around the world in his beautiful home, gave me a tour of his Atlanta Braves office at Turner Field and took me to lunch at Ted's Montana Grill downtown. He's a steak man. All this time, we never talked baseball. We talked about our families and hometowns, our mutual past employment at CNN, our entrepreneurial spirits and, believe it or not, my hopes and dreams.

The last time I saw him is when he said to come visit him in the hospital after foot surgery. His schedule and travel became busy again, and there was no more

Fellow legends and eventual Hall of Famers Willie Mays and Hank Aaron meet at Royals Stadium in Kansas City prior to the All-Star Game in July 1973. (AP Photo)

time for me. But I will never forget the span I spent with the great Hank Aaron, getting to know the man.

ELLEN WEAVER HARTMAN: TAKING HIS TIME

I had the pleasure and honor of working with Hank Aaron for the past 25-plus years. I traveled with Hank all over the country, promoting the Arby's RBI Awards program, opening up his restaurants for Arby's, Church's and Popeyes, including an Arby's in Sheboygan, Wisconsin that was attended by his teammates from the Milwaukee Braves, attending the MLB Awards ceremonies, hosting Olympic baseball teams at his home in 1996 and so many galas and events.

On one trip, Hank and I went for a run near the hotel, and I asked him if he could pick up the pace a bit. Hank said to me, "That's why I hit so many home runs, I wanted to take my time around the bases. I didn't have to be fast." Hank taught me how to live with humility and grace.

MAYNARD HOLBROOK JACKSON III: ALWAYS THERE

Some of my earliest memories center around being taken to Braves baseball games to watch him play and the relationship my parents had with the Aarons. We all lived in southwest Atlanta only minutes from each other and growing up in Atlanta back then felt like the America Dr. King must have dreamed about.

I grew up playing baseball at Adams Park. Just a short distance from where Hank and Billye still have their family home. I remember the excitement of when Mr. Aaron made history, breaking Babe Ruth's record. It was a huge deal in my home. My father and I were there. My mother was giddy with excitement as well. My maternal grandfather, Burnalle "Bun" Hayes, had played in the Negro Leagues for the Jacksonville Red Caps, Baltimore Black Sox, the Brooklyn Dodgers Negro League, so the love for baseball and baseball players is imprinted into my DNA. Watching Mr. Aaron play as a child fueled pure joy for me.

Even beyond Mr. Aaron as a baseball player, he and his wife, Billye have remained cheerleaders for my endeavors. Most recently, when my wife, Wendy, and I decided to make the documentary, "Maynard," about my father, it was Billye and Hank that made the very first donation to get us started. They recognized that my father's story needed to be told and, in their usual fashion, they supported us.

I always found it encouraging that Mr. Aaron had huge successes in life and could have chosen to live anywhere in the world and yet he chose to remain in southwest Atlanta, the community where he knew he had always been protected, loved and respected. Not pretentious and always humble, he kept his friends and family close.

DIANE LOUPE: A TEST DRIVE

When my son was about 10 years old, he read an ad in the newspaper that anyone who went down to the Hank Aaron BMW dealership and took a test drive would get an autographed copy of Mr. Aaron's autobiography. Well, I loved my son, so I agreed to drive him down to Union City to get the book. When we got there, I confessed to the salesman that I wasn't really in the market to buy a BMW, we really just wanted the book. The salesman smiled and asked if we'd like to meet Mr. Aaron.

"He's here?" we asked, amazed. Yep, and the salesman led us into Mr. Aaron's office where he shook my son's hand and spoke to him briefly. I remember he had a chess set on his desk, and the king was Hank Aaron. My son remembers that Babe Ruth was the queen. He spent a few minutes giving my son a lifelong memory of one of the greats.

In fact, my son, Daniel Easley, now works for the Atlanta Braves as a graphic designer. Mr. Aaron was a class act. I mean, he didn't have to spend his time on a kid and his mom who wasn't going to buy a car. But he actually asked my son a few questions about baseball. It wasn't just a perfunctory hello.

MARK TOLBERT: FILLING HANK'S SHOES

As a 16-year-old growing up in Atlanta, I had a dream job. I was a batboy for the Atlanta Braves. Actually, I was batboy for the visiting team. Every team that came to Atlanta to play the Braves over the summer of 1967 had me as their batboy for their games. I wore their uniform, worked in the visiting clubhouse and rubbed shoulders with future Hall of Famers. I played pitch with Willie Mays!

One day, I arrived at the stadium and realized I had left my cleats at home. It was a few hours before game time; most players were not at the stadium yet, so I took the tunnel over to the Braves Clubhouse. I found my friend, the Braves batboy. He was also named Mark and was 16, same as me. I asked if he had an extra pair of cleats I could borrow. He led me over to his locker and offered me his spare pair. I asked, "What size are these?" "Size 8," he said. "I need a size 10," I said. "I can't wear an 8!"

Someone was standing behind us overheard our conversation and said, "I have a pair of 10s you can borrow." It was Hank Aaron! He took me over to his locker and loaned me a pair of his shoes to wear for the game that night, which I did.

I like to tell people, "I can fill Hank Aaron's shoes!" I did … one night … for about four hours. After the game, I shined them and took them back.

To this day, it remains one of my best memories. He did not have to do that, but he did. He probably knew what it would mean to me. He may not have known it would be a story I would tell my grandchildren 54 years later. One of them texted me to tell me the news of his passing. I texted him back: "He was very kind to me 54 years ago! Be kind!"

JAYA FRANKLIN: GETTING HIS FLOWERS

Georgia State University was honoring Mr. Aaron back in 2015 or 2016. I was doing communications for the event, and someone caught me getting a selfie with Mr. Aaron. I was excited to meet him. I knew I was in the presence of greatness. He had accomplished so much beyond baseball in his 86 years on this earth.

Regardless, he was so nice to me, and he took the time to allow me to take a picture of him with my phone. One thing I can say for sure is, he definitely got his flowers while he could still smell them, and that makes me smile.

STEVE ALLEN: PRESENTING 'THE LEGEND'

On April 8, 1974, I was one of the countless millions watching television to see Hank Aaron break Babe Ruth's unbreakable record. I was a 19-year-old Black man, at the time just beginning to find his way in the world. When Mr. Aaron hit number 715, I jumped up and down with unbridled joy. A Black man had done what was considered impossible. He did it in spite of all the obstacles he faced, and I saw it happen from our living room in Raleigh.

At that time, I never dreamed I'd ever meet Mr. Aaron. But, 25 years later, on the anniversary of that momentous occasion, there I was presenting [my painting] "The Legend" to "The Legend." The event was the Chasing the Dream Foundation Gala, and Mr. Aaron's 65th birthday celebration. I am hard-pressed to tell you exactly how I felt at that moment. I can say it was absolutely wonderful, I was on cloud nine.

This presentation of "The Legend" ranked with the unveiling of "Uniting Colors of the World," the official mural I created for the 1996 Atlanta Centennial Olympic Games. To top it all off, "The Legend" now hangs in the Major League Baseball Hall of Fame in Cooperstown. I can truly say Mr. Aaron had a profound effect on my life, first as a young Black male growing up in America and as an artist.

Seeing him and knowing his story, helped me realize I could accomplish great things too. This includes my work with the Olympics and with the Smithsonian Institution NMAAHC. Mr. Aaron blazed a path for me and others to follow; I was truly inspired by his humanity and greatness.

KARVIS JONES: A DREAM COME TRUE

I met Hank Aaron for the first time in June 2016, believe it or not. The only other time I was in the same room with him was on April 8, 2014, on the 40th anniversary where he broke Babe Ruth's home run record, inside a suite at Turner Field. There were so many people in the suite that I only managed to shake hands with his teammate Dusty Baker.

It was a dream come true to meet Hank Aaron because he paved the way for me to enjoy the work that I do in sports broadcasting. As a young person growing up in Holly Springs, Mississippi, I read about Hank Aaron's life in books and magazines, and he was one of my early sports heroes. I'm forever grateful for his life and legacy. Meeting Hank Aaron was my way of saying thank you for his courage and for giving back to the Atlanta community and the nation.

DELBERT JARMON: I CRIED

No huge story, but I was honored to go and meet Hank Aaron a few years ago when he came to Duke University in honor of having a building named after him and his wife, the Hank Aaron & Billye Williams Young Scholars Summer Research Institute.

I was allowed to bring several of my students and my son along with me to meet the legend. It was a very touching moment. I literally cried when I met him.

ADD SEYMOUR: A CHANCE RIDE

I was working at Morehouse in communications on Commencement Sunday a few years ago. It was early, and I was driving a golf cart around to get myself prepared and not shuttling anybody around. But I had to stop at some point, and a woman came over to me and asked if I could give her father a ride to the main part of the campus for commencement.

The first thing I thought was, "Dang! I don't want to get this started with people. That's going to slow me down." But something said, go ahead and do it. Who is going to say no anyway? So I said, "Sure." She got

on the back and, the next thing I know, Hank Aaron climbed into the seat next to me! I was sooooooo blown away and excited. I grew up a Hank Aaron fan. I read everything about him when I was a child. Besides Ali, Aaron was my first sports hero. He was a god to me. I told him that and about my grandfather and I watching him hit 715 when I was 7.

He was so gracious on that short ride and was thanking me. I was so blown away. I said, "No, thank you for everything."

A couple of years later, at Morehouse's Candle in the Dark Gala, I ran into him again. I said, "You remember me? I gave you a ride on my golf cart at Morehouse's commencement." He laughed and said, "I do!"

GREGORY WHITE: RECOGNIZING TRAILBLAZERS

I was able to capture a historical picture of Hank Aaron and James "Red" Moore, a former Atlanta Black Cracker. Hank shared that, if it were not for players like Red Moore, he would never had the opportunity to play in the big leagues.

Hank showed a lot of class and a humble spirit as he took time to take pictures with everyone that evening.

ROSE SCOTT: LOOK OUT FOR MY MOTHER

When you meet your heroes and sheroes, even as a journalist, the inner kid takes over and you can't stop smiling, despite being in awe of someone you've always wanted to meet. That's how I felt when I met Hank Aaron. Interestingly, at the time, I was still trying to find solid footing in this town as a journalist. I was on the path, albeit slow to my heart's desire. I had a weekend job working the front desk at the Landmark Condominiums in downtown Atlanta.

Mr. Aaron's mother lived in the building, and he always came by. We'd talk about sports – of course, baseball – and I bragged about my hometown St. Louis Cardinals. Our conversations were no longer than 10 minutes at a time, but he seemed impressed with

Hank Aaron greets fans from the back of a pickup truck during the Hall of Fame Legends Parade down Main Street in July 2014, in Cooperstown, N.Y. (Curtis Compton/The Atlanta Journal-Constitution)

my knowledge of the Negro Leagues, quite an honor coming from the Hammer. I remarked about the slow pace my career was taking. He told me to "hang in there" and "keep striving." It's kind of like baseball, he said. "But I want you to go beyond home plate. Keep striving." And then, with a smile, he added, "And look out for my mother. Call me anytime."

He gave me his number. I never called, just held onto a number written on the corner end of a torn sheet off a yellow notepad.

Fast forward years later, I'm a reporter and producer in the WABE newsroom. Public Broadcasting Atlanta sponsored a golf team in the annual Morehouse School of Medicine golf tournament, presented in partnership with Hank Aaron. Full disclosure, the PBA golf team consisted of employees who played golf, not golfers – there's a difference. Before the tournament got underway, as I was taking practice swings, I spotted him.

And, when I went up to Mr. Aaron, he said, "Hey, I know you," and we laughed. I proudly exclaimed where I was working and what I was doing, as if I was telling my own father. I wanted him to know how much I appreciated the encouraging words. Also, we both admitted golf was fun, but clearly we were better at other sports. I'll never forget his kindness.

MARK KAHN: UNASSUMING

I grew up in Savannah and used to regularly attend Savannah Braves games in the '70s and early '80s as a kid. Savannah was then the AA affiliate of the Braves. In the early '80s, I went to a Savannah game, and Hank Aaron was at the game in his front office capacity for the big club. I was about 12 years old.

Savannah Braves games were not particularly well-attended then, as the stadium (Grayson Stadium) was pretty rundown. It was unusual for attendance to exceed 1,000 on a non-giveaway night. As a result,

125

Hank wasn't getting a lot of attention.

I went up to him during the game and asked for his autograph, which he happily gave. Like I said, not much to the story – but I think it was pretty typical – just a generous and unassuming soul.

FRED BUNDY: HOW ABOUT A BEER?

I worked in the visiting clubhouse at Atlanta Stadium in 1969 and 1970. In addition to clubhouse duties, I was the left field ball boy in '69 and batboy in '70. I had several interactions with the Hammer. The most memorable for me was on the night the Braves won the division title in '69. Despite our boss, Bill Acree, telling us kids after the game to stay in the visiting clubhouse and not go over to the Braves clubhouse.

I didn't listen and went over anyway to witness the celebration. The Hammer was being interviewed at his locker by numerous reporters. He spotted me in my Braves uniform and asked if we still had beer in our clubhouse.

Apparently, the Braves had gone through theirs celebrating. I dashed over to the visiting clubhouse, washed out a milk jug and filled it with draft beer. I went out of the dugout and walked to where home plate had been (celebratory fans had dug it up), sat down and took a couple of swallows before proceeding back into the Braves clubhouse. I marched straight through the crowd to deliver the Hammer his request. He was very happy. However, I cannot say the same for my boss.

DAVE HAMRIN: 'HEY, HAM'

My dad was on a flight to Sarasota that Hank Aaron was on. He introduced himself and asked Hank if he'd help pull a prank on the guy who was picking my dad up at the airport. My dad told Hank that he and his friend were big baseball fans (true). He asked Hank Aaron to pretend that he and my dad were old friends.

Dad mentioned that his friends all called him "Ham" (also true). Anyway, when my dad landed he told his friend that he had never mentioned it before, but he and Hank Aaron were old friends and that Hank was on the flight with my dad. My dad's friend just shook his head in disbelief. But, as dad and his friend were picking up my dad's luggage, they heard a booming voice yelling, "Hey, Ham! See you later, buddy!"

It was Hank Aaron, smiling and waving, just like an old friend would do. So, I've always thought Hank Aaron was a pretty great guy. My dad's friend was quite impressed. My dad 'fessed up on the drive home.

CAROLYN S. CARLSON: 'MAY I MOVE YOUR CAR?'

I'm a huge baseball fan, especially a Braves fan, and held Hank Aaron in awe. So, I was thrilled when Atlanta mayoral candidate Marvin Arrington told me Aaron was a neighbor and friend, and that he would vote for and with Arrington on voting day in the 1997 mayoral race. I was Arrington's press secretary, so I contacted all the TV stations, and they dutifully showed up at the Cascade Road area polling place at 6:45 a.m.

We had arranged for Arrington to be the first to vote, and Aaron walked up a few minutes before the polls opened. Arrington was introducing him to me and others when a police officer came up to tell Aaron he had to move his car. It was parked illegally and blocking the emergency lane. This news came, of course, just as the poll manager was waving them in.

I jumped in front of them and asked, "May I move your car for you?" He looked at Arrington, who nodded, and with some relief, he handed me his keys. It was a very nice luxury car, a top-of-the-line BMW, if I remember correctly, so you can bet I drove very carefully to a legal parking place.

I ran back to the polling place door in time to watch the two emerge and to hand Aaron his keys. Ever the gentleman, he politely thanked me. I didn't ask for an autograph, though I thought of it. But I've cherished the unusual encounter ever since.

BRAD GAINES: A TIMELY AUTOGRAPH

I grew up in middle Tennessee. I turned 13 in 1974 when he broke the home run record. I vividly remember listening to the Braves games on my little portable radio to see how many home runs Hank would hit each night. I laid in bed late at night many times, listening to their games when they were playing on the West Coast.

Fortunately, we were able to watch those April 1974 games on television when he tied and broke the record. Then I was fortunate enough to have my parents take me to "Hank Aaron Day" at Fulton County Stadium, in July 1974, where I got a poster.

I kept it rolled up nice and neat until 1987. That year, Mr. Aaron came to Nashville on one of his autograph tours, and I was lucky enough to meet him and have him sign my poster. He was without a doubt the most gracious person that I have ever met.

He let us take as many pictures as we wanted and even shook my hand! I will never forget that day.

CRAIG CAMUSO: AN AURA OF ROYALTY

I was almost 7 years old when I attended the Braves' game on April 8, 1974, and witnessed history. My dad had secured us pretty good seats in the lower upper deck between the first base dugout and home plate to see Aaron break Babe Ruth's home run record. Prior to that, but certainly afterward, began my fandom of the Hammer. I even had the 45 record "Move Over Babe, Here Comes Henry" that I played over and over and can still hum the song to this day.

I was able to meet Aaron for the first time in the early '90s, when I attended a card show and got him to sign (along with Willie Mays and Mickey Mantle) a picture that I still have. It wasn't a long conversation, as there were many others there also wanting an autograph, but he was just as gentle and modest as all the stories about him have been.

But it was the opening night of SunTrust Park that I was really able to meet him. Two friends and

I had tickets to the game, which had a playoff-type atmosphere in the brand-new ballpark. We knew there were several dignitaries in the owner's box because one of the friends with us worked for someone who was seated there. We followed him down to the area and remained quiet while he convinced the bodyguards for Governor Deal, President Carter and several others that he had been summoned down by his boss and we were with him.

They let us in. As we wandered into the box, seated in the back row over to the right was Aaron. As soon as I saw him, I forgot where I was and who else was in the box. I made an immediate beeline straight to Aaron. He kinda chuckled at me as I rambled on about being there as a kid when he hit 715 and that he was the real home run king and would it be OK if I could get a picture.

He obliged, and I handed my camera to one of the other friends and knelt beside him with that huge smile on my face. He had the aura of royalty, not by the way he acted, but just by his sheer presence. He chatted with me for a couple of minutes before I realized I was keeping him from watching the game. ◗